THE MICHAEL FIELD EGG COOKBOOK

ALSO BY MICHAEL FIELD

Michael Field's Cooking School
Culinary Classics and Improvisations
All Manner of Food
Cooking with Michael Field
(edited by Joan Scobey)

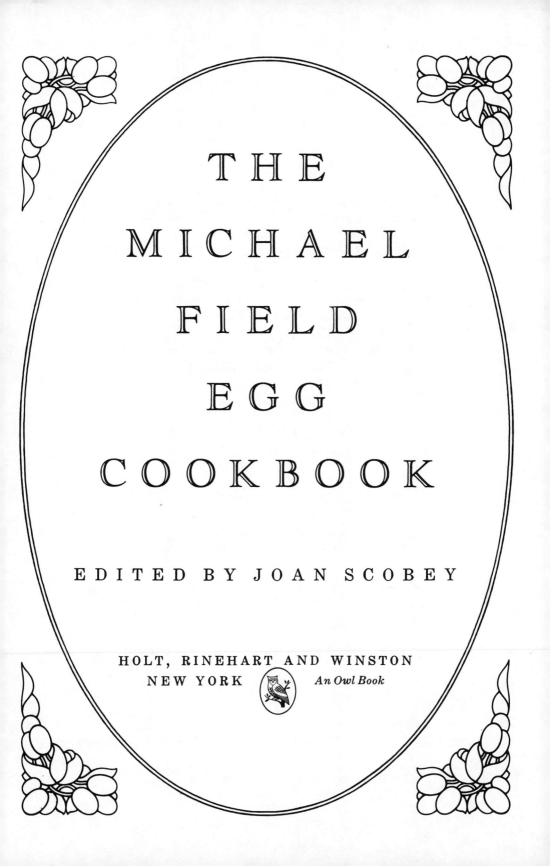

THE

MICHAEL

FIELD

EGG

COOKBOOK

EDITED BY JOAN SCOBEY

HOLT, RINEHART AND WINSTON
NEW YORK · An Owl Book

First published in February 1981 by Holt, Rinehart and Winston,
383 Madison Avenue,
New York, New York 10017.
Published simultaneously in Canada by Holt, Rinehart and
Winston of Canada, Limited.

Library of Congress Cataloging in Publication Data
Field, Michael, 1915–1971.
The Michael Field egg cookbook.
"An Owl book."
Includes index.
1. Cookery (Eggs).   I. Scobey, Joan.   II. Title.
TX745.F47   641.6'75   80–13655
ISBN 0–03–048221–6

First Edition

Designer: Joy Chu
Printed in the United States of America
1   3   5   7   9   10   8   6   4   2

FOR JONATHAN AND FRANCES

CONTENTS

A Personal Note

Michael Field's intent, as writer and teacher, was to instruct his students in the basic skills of cooking, not merely to furnish them with recipes, however imaginative and reliable those recipes are. His interest in food involved taste, in both its senses. He brought his impeccable sense of taste to all the recipes he created—not only to the finished dish, which was, of course, to taste superb, but also to the recipe and its origins. Taste, for him, involved integrity—respect for ingredients, tradition, and sound culinary skills. He appreciated modest peasant fare as well as elegant and elaborate cuisines. He gave as much thought to preparing a proper pancake as to baking a gossamer soufflé. And his concern that both kinds of dishes be produced with the same meticulous care is honored in this book.

With few exceptions, the success of most of the recipes in this book depends, for one reason or another, on the hen's bounty—whole eggs, egg whites, and/or egg yolks. Field was rather partial to the miraculous egg. "Eggs are not only one of the most delectable of foods with magical powers when combined with other foods," he wrote, "but nutritional powerhouses as well. Because an egg contains protein of the highest quality, all the essential vitamins (except vitamin C), saturated and unsaturated fatty acids, a preponderance of important minerals and a minimum of carbohydrates, the egg is, as it were, an almost complete food, with the added advantage of averaging only 72 calories." Today nutritionists have come to appreciate these qualities, and most nutritional plans include a moderate number of eggs a week.

Whatever the rate of consumption, the best possible culinary use should be made of this miraculous food. And because eggs transform themselves into such diverse creations and because few other foods are as dependent on a precise sense of timing, egg cookery commands the attention of all serious cooks.

All the recipes and glossary information are by Michael Field. Most come from the cookbook series that was available only to members of the Doubleday Book Clubs. Although Michael Field intended to use those eight volumes as the basis for a new cookbook, he died before he was able to produce it. The major portion of that material appears in *Cooking with Michael Field*; the remainder is included in this book. In several recipes, I have taken the liberty of adding food processor techniques when that seemed helpful to the completion of the recipe. Although food processors were not in common use when Field devised and tested these recipes, I am confident that, had they been, he would have made good use of them.

Michael Field always dedicated his books to his family, and in his name I continue that tradition. Had he lived, I believe he would also have liked to acknowledge Helen McCully and Mary McCabe Gandall for their work on the original volumes, and Jean Anderson and Helen Witty for their editorial contributions to the original series. For myself, I am indebted to the generosity of Edward A. Fogel, and to my editor, Marian S. Wood, who shares my admiration for the meticulous hand and inventive soul of that extraordinary Master Cook, Michael Field.

Joan Scobey

THE MICHAEL FIELD EGG COOKBOOK

Equipment and Utensils

The following equipment and utensils are used to prepare the specific recipes in this book.

Kitchen Appliances

Electric mixer. My preference is a large heavy-duty mixer that has among its attachments a large balloon-like whip that can whip egg whites to great heights.

Electric blender. Electric blenders simplify the making of soufflés and mousses because they purée, pulverize, grate, crumb, and blend foods with equal ease and speed. Latest models have push-button controls and a variety of speeds for specific jobs, but an older model with only a low and a high speed works successfully.

Food processor. These new "miracle" machines, of the type originated by Cuisinart, have taken over most of the functions of the electric blender and have added a few of their own: they shred, slice, and julienne vegetables, grind meat, and chop just about everything, all almost instantaneously. They come with chopping and mixing blades and all kinds of slicing and shredding disks, usually at a relatively high price.

Waffle iron. Unless you are an avid collector of antiques or a frequent traveler to Europe, you will discover that it is virtually impossible to find a top-of-the-stove waffle iron. The waffle irons available in America are electric ones, and most of the recent models have a nonstick baking surface. You can find them in a variety of shapes—square, oblong, or round—and the one you choose is really a matter of taste. I caution you to follow the manufacturer's instructions carefully.

It may interest you to know that a combination griddle and waffle maker is also available. For reasons of economy, this appliance has its advantages, but if you are impatient by nature, you may find it exasperating to cope with having to reverse the grids. However, its performance as either waffle iron or griddle is perfectly satisfactory.

Griddle. You can choose from an array of griddles, from the most elaborate to the simplest.

ELECTRIC GRIDDLES. These are comparatively expensive, but from my point of view they are a good investment. They are equipped with thermostats that enable you to bake your pancakes at exactly the temperature you want, which the thermostat will maintain throughout the baking. Most electric griddles have a nonstick coating that prevents pancakes from sticking whether it is greased or not. Buy a griddle with the largest, flattest cooking surface you can find—avoid those with a surface that slopes down perceptibly at the sides. Whatever brand you buy, carefully read the manufacturer's instructions for its care and use.

ELECTRIC FRYING PANS. This appliance, like the griddle, is regulated by a thermostat. Although smaller in area than most electric griddles, these pans are quite satisfactory for baking three or four pancakes at a time. The shallower the pan, the easier it will be to turn the pancakes. Again, I would recommend a pan with a nonstick lining.

BUILT-IN RANGE GRIDDLES. Many of the newer ranges, both gas and electric, come equipped with griddles, most of them with a nonstick coating. Some are built-ins and others are designed to be set in place over an extra burner. The more versatile range griddles have temperature settings controlled by a thermostat. Follow the manufacturer's recommendations for temperature settings, then experiment to find the heat level that will bake pancakes as you like them.

TOP-OF-THE-STOVE GRIDDLES. If you do not own an electric griddle or frying pan, a top-of-the-stove griddle will do very well. You may choose one that is round, square, or oblong, and either large or small. The traditional kind is made of cast iron; newer types are made of heavy aluminum and have a nonstick coating. Because you will have to control its heat manually, a stove-top griddle demands constant vigilance on your part, and your success with them will require considerable skill. However, with experience, you can use a top-of-the-stove griddle successfully.

Pots, Pans, and Baking and Serving Dishes

Double boiler. The inset (top pan) should be of 1½- to 2-quart capacity. Stainless steel is ideal, but it is expensive and sometimes difficult to find. Considerably less expensive enameled pans, while they may chip and tend to be lightweight, can be quite satisfactory. Avoid aluminum pans, which will discolor sauces containing egg yolks and certain acid ingredients like wine, and Pyrex glass double boilers, which are not only breakable but retain heat so persistently that they make cooking control difficult.

Heavy saucepans with tight-fitting covers. Pans of enameled cast iron, stainless steel, or tin-lined heavy copper are all satisfactory. For making soufflé base sauces, mousses, and custards, you will find the 1- or 1½-quart, the 2-quart, and the 3- or 4-quart sizes most useful and practical.

10-inch sauté pan. Usually made of heavy-duty cast aluminum (avoid black cast iron), this is the classic pan (in French, a *sautoir*) used by professional cooks. The one I recommend is made by Wear-Ever. It has straight sides, is 2¼ inches deep, and is unlined.

Heavy frying pans with tight-fitting covers. The best domestic pans are made of heavyweight aluminum and have sloping sides and nonstick linings. Attractive and useful imported enameled cast-iron pans are also available, but they tend to be quite expensive. You will need three sizes: an 8-inch pan with 6-inch bottom; a 10-inch pan with 8-inch bottom; and a 12-inch pan with 10-inch bottom.

6½-inch crêpe pan (5-inch bottom). This small-size crêpe pan, called No. 16 in the trade, may be difficult to find in housewares stores, but quality department stores, kitchen specialty shops, and restaurant-supply houses should have them.

Jelly-roll pan. This should be a sturdy aluminum pan, about 16 by 11 by ½ inch. They are available with or without a nonstick lining.

Baking sheet. The best baking sheets are made of heavy-grade aluminum and measure about 18 inches long and 14 inches wide.

Soufflé dishes or molds. The straight-sided porcelain soufflé dishes, the new glass soufflé molds, and the plain round metal molds known as charlottes are multipurpose containers, interchangeable for making soufflés, mousses, and creams. You will need the 1-, 1½-, and 2-quart sizes.

Ramekins or custard cups. For making individual soufflés or shirred eggs, the 6-ounce size, about 4 inches in diameter, is best. Porcelain ramekins, either plain or decorated, can go gracefully from oven to table, but the old-fashioned custard cups, which are less expensive and less attractive, can also be used.

Roasting pan. Certain creams and custards are baked in a hot-water bath (bain-marie) to keep them from curdling. I have found an all-purpose roasting pan measuring about 16 by 11 by 3 inches to be an ideal size for a water bath.

Ring molds. Plain molds in 4- to 5-cup and 6-cup sizes made of heavy-grade aluminum or tin-lined copper are best for molding cold mousses and creams.

Fish mold. Fish mousses are especially glamorous when made in a fish-shaped mold. I recommend a 3-cup capacity. These molds are made of either heavy aluminum or tin-lined copper. The aluminum molds, by far the less expensive, are available in housewares sections of most department stores. The copper molds, usually imported from France, Italy, or Portugal, are obtainable at most gourmet or kitchen specialty shops.

Scallop shells (coquilles). These seashells give individual seafood soufflés a glamorous look. Most shells measure from 4½ to 5 inches across the top and are sold in sets of a dozen or half dozen in many housewares departments and specialty kitchen shops. They are not expensive, and they can be used again and again.

Large flameproof platter. This platter is indispensable for baking omelet soufflés and, for best results, should be made of heavy-duty silver plate, porcelain, or ceramic ware that will transmit the oven heat slowly and evenly. I find a platter measuring about 15 inches long and 12 inches wide a perfect size for most omelet soufflés.

Baking-and-serving dishes. One useful dish for the recipes in this book is approximately 2 inches deep, 12 to 14 inches long, and 8 or 9 inches wide. It can be made of tin-lined copper, enameled cast iron, pottery, or ovenproof glass. Ideally, the dish should be attractive enough to bring to the table for serving.

Other useful sizes are dishes about 8 inches square, about 9 inches in diameter, and a 1-quart flameproof baking dish for making crème brûlée, which is taken straight from refrigerator to broiler and must be able to take the abrupt heat change without cracking.

Serving bowls. Dessert mousses and creams that are too soft to unmold can be chilled in their own serving dish. Because such desserts are often colorful, a crystal or glass bowl will show them off to best advantage. The two most useful sizes are 1- to 1½-quart and 2-quart dishes.

Parfait glasses. Certain frozen mousses look spectacular in tall, tapering crystal parfait glasses. Tulip-shaped wine goblets—the 8-ounce size—are equally showy.

Cutting and Chopping

Chopping board. The most useful have a cutting surface of polyethylene, which won't chip or retain odors, or of durable hardwood like maple.

Knives. They can be made of carbon steel or stainless steel but must be of high quality to take a sharp cutting edge; get the best you can afford. Stainless steel resists most stains; carbon steel holds its cutting edge longer but stains and rusts easily. You will need a small sharp paring knife, about 3 inches long; a medium-size utility knife, about 5 inches long; and a heavy 10-inch French chef's knife or an 8-inch chopping knife.

Knife sharpener. Among the best is the Zip-Zap, which is made of special ceramic and looks like a miniature sharpening steel.

Food mill. This round, hand-cranked mill fits snugly over small mixing bowls and saucepans and purées soft foods such as berries and other fruits easily and efficiently. Some models have removable disks for fine, medium, and coarse puréeing.

Food chopper. Because of the delicacy of soufflés and mousses, the foods incorporated into the base sauces should be as finely ground or minced as possible. A sturdy food chopper that clamps securely to the counter top is indispensable for grinding meats.

Potato ricer. This eliminates the need for peeling potatoes that are to be mashed.

Stand-up four-sided grater.

Rotary-type (Mouli) grater. This is available with fine and coarse shredders and a slicing cylinder, and is useful for grinding hard cheeses and nuts.

Vegetable peeler with swivel-action blade.

Zester and/or citrus peeler. Use the first to remove strips and the second to shred fine pieces of citrus rind without the underlying bitter pith.

Measuring Utensils

Timer. It should mark minutes and a few hours.

Measuring spoons. A set of four holds 1 tablespoon and 1, ½, and ¼ teaspoon.

Stainless-steel measuring cups. For measuring dry ingredients, cups should hold 1, ½, ⅓, and ¼ cup.

Ovenproof glass measuring cups. For measuring liquids and batter, the most useful are the pint (2-cup) and quart (4-cup) sizes. The newer ones include a liter scale.

Ladles. Graduated sets of stainless-steel measuring ladles ranging from 2 tablespoons to 1 cup in capacity are available; the 2-ounce (¼-cup) size is most useful for these recipes. Although ladles make the task of measuring batter easier, they are not indispensable.

Oven thermometer. It is worth the small investment to buy an oven thermometer. Always test the oven temperature each time you cook, and place the thermometer as near as possible to the baking dish without touching it.

Candy thermometer. The type of candy thermometer I prefer is encased in stainless steel, with a bulb guard that keeps the sensor of the thermometer from touching the side or bottom of the pan. It is fairly easy to read, and its stem need only be immersed 1 inch in the liquid for a reliable reading.

Mixing bowls. A set of three is recommended—small, medium, and large—preferably of stainless steel, heavy heatproof glass, or ceramic ware, but definitely not aluminum, which may discolor the eggs.

Colander. Buy the largest size you can find, and make sure it is the stand-up type that rests on three legs.

Wooden spoons.

Wooden spatulas. They resemble spoons but have a flat oval blade in place of a bowl and are excellent for mixing.

Long-handled metal spoons, slotted and unslotted.

Metal spatulas, wide and narrow, slotted and unslotted. Spatulas with an angle between the blade and the handle, and with a blade at least 6 inches long, as well as a flat spatula, are useful.

Rubber spatulas, wide and narrow.

Kitchen tongs. I recommend tongs approximately 8 inches long, preferably with smooth rather than serrated clamps.

Wire whisks or whips. Small and medium-size wire whisks or whips are indispensable for making soufflé base sauces, for incorporating small amounts of beaten egg whites into soufflé bases, and for countless other mixing, stirring, and beating jobs.

Balloon whip. Called *fouet* in French, this large wire whip inflates egg whites to spectacular volume.

Large copper bowl. If you are using a balloon whip to beat egg whites, a large copper bowl produces the most volume.

Rotary or electric beater. Although many French chefs prefer to whip egg whites or heavy cream with the balloon whip, I have found that a good rotary or electric beater simplifies the task and does just as effective a job.

Pastry bag and tips. These are available in sizes from 10 to 24 inches; the most useful is a 16-inch one. For piping whipped cream, a canvas bag is preferable to nylon; canvas takes a firm hold on the whipped cream and gives you more control as you pipe it out.

The sizes and patterns of pastry tips are designated by name and number. Try to buy a complete set of decorative and plain tips. If you must limit your purchase, settle for Star Tip No. 9 and Plain Tips Nos. 3, 6, and 9.

Fine-meshed sieves, large, medium, and small sizes. Sieves are indispensable for straining sauces and custards, puréeing fruits and vegetables, and dusting the tops of soufflés, mousses, pancakes, and crêpes with finely grated cheese, confectioners' sugar, cocoa, or fine dry crumbs.

Sifter.

Duster. You will find a small, inexpensive aluminum shaker with a removable perforated top an invaluable aid for sprinkling powdered sugar on pancakes, crêpes, and soufflés, although a fine-meshed sieve will do the same job.

Pastry brushes.

Cake tester. This small skewerlike device is much handier than the traditional toothpick.

Bulb baster. Select a sturdy stainless-steel baster, which is as effective in removing grease from pan drippings as it accumulates as it is for basting.

Pepper mills. You need one for black pepper, one for white pepper, both with adjustable grinding mechanisms.

Nutmeg grater.

Lobster pick.

Cheesecloth. This is for lining sieves and colanders when sauces are to be finely strained.

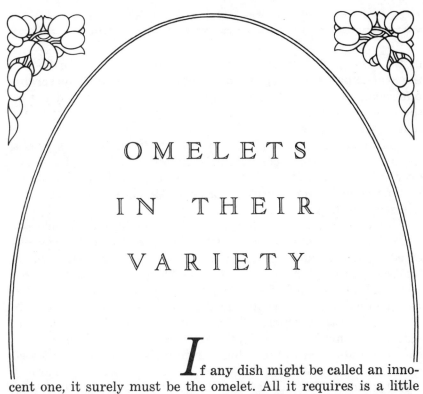

OMELETS

IN THEIR

VARIETY

*I*f any dish might be called an inno-
cent one, it surely must be the omelet. All it requires is a little
butter, a couple of eggs, a fork, a frying pan, and, at the very
most, two minutes of your time. In the face of these incontrovert-
ible facts, you may wonder why so few cooks, however expert they
may be in other culinary areas, can make an omelet successfully.
As always, success or near-failure is purely a matter of technique,
plus an understanding of what an omelet really is.

There are two schools of thought about omelets, and the one
point upon which they agree is that an omelet can be made well
only in a heavy omelet pan, which must *never* be washed and,
heaven forbid, must never be used to cook anything else. From
this point on, hostilities begin.

The first school of omelet makers pours the beaten eggs into
the heated and buttered pan, then continuously pushes the outer
edges of the eggs toward the center of the pan as they cook, thus
allowing the uncooked eggs to flow into the newly vacated spaces.
This method is amateurish, because the resulting omelet will almost inevitably be tough and leathery.

Members of the second group make what the French call an
omelette brouillée, or what might be called in English a scrambled omelet. It has a most velvety texture because of the air incorporated into it as the eggs are cooked.

The classic method is to stir the eggs constantly with a fork as they cook, while sliding the pan rapidly back and forth over the heat to prevent the eggs from sticking to the pan. This scrambling maneuver is a difficult one indeed, and before the advent of the nonstick frying pan it was almost impossible for many amateur cooks to master.

My technique for making scrambled French omelets uses a pan with a nonstick surface and eliminates the sliding of the pan over the burner. After a little experience you will find yourself making omelet after omelet like a professional and none of them will stick to the pan.

Among the recipes in this section are some for puffy omelets— what the French call soufflé omelets—in which the eggs are separated, the yolks and whites beaten separately, and then folded together. Although the cooking of a soufflé omelet is a simple process, folding the finished omelet properly requires some practice.

You will have no trouble at all making the egg dish the Italians call a *frittata*, which is flat and never rolled. For *frittata*, the most simply made of omelets, the eggs, combined with vegetables, cheese, croutons, or in fact whatever you wish, are simply allowed to cook undisturbed until they are done. The Italians generally turn the omelet over to fry the other side, but it's preferable to put the almost-cooked omelet under the broiler. The puffing that results makes the *frittata* impressive enough to serve on almost any occasion.

Ingredients for Omelets

Eggs. The flavor—and hence the freshness—of eggs is most important in omelets. Buy the freshest ones you can. Try to find a source of dated eggs, and buy eggs that have been kept under refrigeration. Needless to say, refrigerate them again at home.

Eggs for omelets can be at room temperature or straight from the refrigerator; their temperature before cooking will make no difference in the quality of the omelet.

Butter. Butter, and butter only, is the fat to use for cooking an omelet in the French manner. Unsalted (sweet) butter is best for scrambled and puffed omelets.

Olive oil. Olive oil is preferable to butter for cooking an Italian omelet (*frittata*), which is cooked longer, and in a different fashion, than the French omelet.

Liquids. I prefer not to add any kind of liquid to the eggs for an omelet, not even a little water, although some respectable cooks do. I especially avoid milk and cream, which will toughen the texture of an omelet.

Techniques for Making Omelets

Omelet size. Despite the advice in some cookbooks that you make plain (French) omelets large enough to serve two or even several people, I emphatically advise against it. For perfect plain, puffed, or filled French omelets, the size to make is the individual omelet, cooked in a minute or more. If you are making omelets for several people, you may combine the ingredients, as long as you cook each omelet individually. Techniques for multiple omelets are described on pages 12–13 and 18–20. My Italian omelets, however, may be made in larger sizes with complete success.

Warming the plates. Omelets should be served on plates that are warm but not sizzling; you don't want the omelet to continue cooking on the plate. Before making an omelet, turn the oven to its lowest temperature setting and place the serving plates in it to warm them. Or, warm the plates in your dishwasher at the plate-warming setting.

Beating the eggs. Use a table fork to beat the eggs for both a scrambled omelet and an Italian omelet. Do not use a whisk or a rotary beater, or the eggs will quickly become frothy and the omelet will not have the proper consistency.

On the other hand, for a puffed omelet, a rotary beater is the most satisfactory tool for beating egg whites to their maximum volume.

Heating the butter. It is of crucial importance that the melted butter be at the correct temperature when the uncooked eggs are poured into the omelet pan. For a scrambled French omelet, the butter should have begun to color ever so faintly and give off a slightly nutty aroma. The signal for a puffed omelet is somewhat different. Because puffed omelets take longer to cook than scrambled omelets, in order to eliminate the danger that the butter will burn, the eggs should be poured into the pan just as soon as the butter has melted but before it has begun to color.

Serving the omelets. An omelet must go directly from its pan to a warmed plate and be served at once. Because an omelet will continue to cook internally as it waits, any delay can ruin its delicate texture irretrievably.

SCRAMBLED FRENCH OMELETS

These omelets should always be made individually, as described below. To make several omelets in succession, just increase the quantity of ingredients proportionately. Combine all the eggs and salt in a large mixing bowl and measure out ½ cup of the beaten eggs for each omelet. Then butter the omelet pan again and beat the remaining eggs for a second or two before making each succeeding omelet.

SERVES 1

2 eggs
⅛ teaspoon salt
1 tablespoon butter, softened at room temperature

Preparing the eggs. Break the eggs into a small glass or stainless-steel mixing bowl and add the salt. With a table fork, beat the eggs vigorously for about 30 seconds, or only long enough to combine them.

Cooking the omelet. Spoon about half the softened butter into an 8-inch frying pan with a nonstick surface. Set the pan over medium heat and let the butter melt slowly, tipping the pan from side to side so that the butter spreads evenly over the bottom and sides of the pan. When the butter begins to color and gives off a slightly nutty aroma, quickly pour in the eggs.

With the back of your fork, begin stirring the eggs at once, sweeping the flat of the fork around the circumference of the pan and making ever smaller circles until you reach the center. Almost instantly the eggs will begin to form uneven, soft, but still liquid curds. This entire process should take about 30 seconds or less. While the eggs are still slightly liquid, with the back of your fork quickly and evenly spread them to fill in any gaps so that the surface of the omelet resembles a moist pancake.

Rolling the omelet. Without waiting a moment, grasp the handle of the pan securely and hold it at a slight angle so that the edge of the pan rests lightly on the rim of a warmed serving plate. Slide your fork under the edge of the omelet near the handle and, an inch or so at a time, gently fold the omelet over and over, continuing to roll it until a section only about ½ inch wide remains exposed. Now use the fork to help you slide the omelet out of the pan, while at the same time making the last roll onto the plate. **Serving the omelet.** Brush the surface of the omelet with the remaining softened butter, using a pastry brush. Serve the omelet at once.

VARIATION: FILLED FRENCH OMELETS

Although there is no need whatsoever to fill a scrambled French omelet, a filling can be added just before rolling the omelet. The possible variations are imposing: fresh herbs, or grated cheese; bits of fish, poultry, meat, or vegetables, often creamed and always cooked or warmed separately first.

In the fillings that follow, quantities are for individual omelets. Multiply the quantities of ingredients if you are making several omelets.

Herbed omelet. After beating the eggs, stir in 1 tablespoon of finely chopped fresh parsley, chives, dill, tarragon, chervil, or other herbs, either alone or in any combination you prefer.

Cheese omelet. Just before rolling the omelet, sprinkle the surface evenly with 2 teaspoons of freshly grated Parmesan or Switzerland cheese, or natural sharp Cheddar-type cheese.

Bacon omelet. Just before rolling the omelet, sprinkle it with 2 tablespoons of coarsely crumbled crisp-cooked bacon.

Crouton omelet. Before making the omelet, prepare ¼ cup croutons as described on page 17. Drain them on paper towels, and just before rolling the omelet, scatter them evenly over the surface.

Mushroom omelet. Before making the omelet, prepare the mushroom filling described in the recipe on page 50. Just before rolling the omelet, spread the surface with about 1 tablespoon of filling.

Chicken liver omelet. Before making the omelet, prepare the chicken liver filling described in the recipe on page 53. Just before rolling the omelet, spread the surface with about 1 tablespoon of filling.

Lobster omelet. Before making the omelet, prepare the lobster filling described in the recipe on page 41. Just before rolling the omelet, spread it with about 1 tablespoon of filling.

Crabmeat omelet. Before making the omelet, prepare the crabmeat filling described in the recipe on page 44. Just before rolling the omelet, spread it with about 1 tablespoon of filling.

Shrimp omelet. Before making the omelet, prepare the shrimp filling described in the recipe on page 47. Just before rolling the omelet, spread it with about 1 tablespoon of filling.

VARIATION: SCRAMBLED FRENCH OMELETS WITH RED CAVIAR AND SOUR CREAM

Here is a red caviar and sour cream sauce that is not rolled in the omelet but is served as an accompaniment.

SERVES 4

The Caviar and Sour Cream Sauce
1 cup sour cream
2 tablespoons finely chopped scallions, including about 2 inches of their green tops
2 tablespoons finely chopped fresh parsley
1 tablespoon finely cut fresh dill or 1 teaspoon dried dill weed
½ teaspoon strained fresh lemon juice
Freshly ground black pepper
¼ cup red caviar (2-ounce jar)

The Omelets
8 eggs
½ teaspoon salt
4 tablespoons butter, softened at room temperature

Making the sauce. In a small mixing bowl combine the sour cream, scallions, parsley, dill, lemon juice, and a few grindings of black pepper. With a rubber spatula, stir the ingredients together thoroughly. Then gently stir in the caviar.

Taste the sauce for seasoning. If you prefer a more piquant flavor, add a few more drops of lemon juice and perhaps an extra grinding of black pepper.

Making, rolling, and serving the omelets. Make four individual scrambled French omelets, according to the recipe on page 12. As each omelet is rolled onto its warmed serving plate, spoon about 2 heaping tablespoons of the caviar sauce beside it and serve at once.

ITALIAN OMELET WITH ZUCCHINI AND PARMESAN CHEESE

In Italy an omelet, or *frittata,* is always flat, often served at room temperature, and is very good indeed whether eaten hot or cold. It can also be cut into 1- or 2-inch squares, each square topped with a rolled caper-stuffed anchovy or a sprinkling of finely chopped fresh parsley, and, with great success, served either hot or at room temperature as cocktail accompaniments. *Frittata* also makes an unusual addition to a picnic hamper.

SERVES 4

The Omelet
¼ cup flour
½ teaspoon salt
½ pound small zucchini, unpeeled but washed, dried, trimmed, and cut into ½-inch dice (about 1 cup)
6 eggs
Freshly ground black pepper
4 tablespoons olive oil

The Topping
3 tablespoons freshly grated Parmesan cheese

Preheating the broiler. Set the broiling pan about 4 inches from the source of heat and preheat the broiler at its highest setting for 15 minutes.
Flouring the zucchini. Pour the flour and ¼ teaspoon of the salt into a plastic bag or a sturdy brown paper bag. Drop in the diced zucchini, close the bag tightly, and shake it vigorously until the pieces of zucchini are well floured.

To remove excess flour, pour the contents of the bag into a sieve and shake over a sheet of wax paper. Set the sieve of flour-coated zucchini aside.
Preparing the eggs. Break the eggs into a medium-size mixing bowl and add the remaining ¼ teaspoon of salt and a few grindings of black pepper. Beat the eggs with a table fork for about 30 seconds, or only long enough to combine them.

Frying the zucchini. Pour the olive oil into a 10-inch frying pan with a nonstick surface. Use a pan that can go under the broiler. Set the pan over medium heat on the range. When the oil begins to appear slightly watery, drop in the floured zucchini.

Turning the pieces constantly with a wooden spoon or a spatula, fry the zucchini cubes for about 2 minutes, or until they are lightly browned. Immediately lower the heat and cover the pan. Cook the zucchini for 1 minute more. Then turn the pieces over once or twice, re-cover the pan, and cook the zucchini for a moment longer. The zucchini will have softened somewhat, but the pieces should still retain their shape.

Making the omelet and broiling the top. Stir the beaten eggs once or twice and pour them over the zucchini. With a spatula, spread the zucchini as evenly as possible throughout the eggs.

Still over low heat, let the omelet cook for 4 to 5 minutes, lifting up an edge of the omelet with the spatula after about 3 minutes to see how quickly the bottom is browning. Adjust the heat if necessary. When the underside is golden brown and the top is still somewhat liquid, scatter the Parmesan cheese evenly over the omelet.

Without waiting a second, slide the pan under the preheated broiler. Broil the omelet for about 2 minutes, checking it constantly. As soon as the top has puffed and turned a speckled golden brown, remove the pan from the broiler.

Serving the omelet. With the spatula, free the edges of the omelet from the sides of the pan. Then, grasping the handle of the pan firmly, tilt the pan at a 45-degree angle and let the omelet slide flat onto a warmed round platter. Serve the omelet at once, or later, at room temperature, cutting it into wedges at the table.

VARIATION: ITALIAN OMELET WITH ARTICHOKE HEARTS AND PARMESAN CHEESE

Another version of the Italian omelet can be made by substituting 1 cup of frozen artichoke hearts for the zucchini. After thoroughly defrosting the artichoke hearts, cut them in half, pat them dry with paper towels, and coat them with flour as described in the preceding recipe. Fry the artichoke hearts and make the omelet in precisely the same way as the zucchini omelet.

ITALIAN OMELET WITH CROUTONS AND MOZZARELLA CHEESE

SERVES 4

The Omelet
6 eggs
½ teaspoon salt
½ teaspoon crumbled dried oregano
Freshly ground black pepper
½ cup mozzarella cheese cut into ¼-inch cubes
5 tablespoons olive oil
1 cup bread cubes about ½-inch size, without crusts

The Topping
3 tablespoons freshly grated Parmesan cheese

Preheating the broiler. Set the broiling pan about 4 inches from the source of heat and preheat the broiler at its highest setting for about 15 minutes.
Preparing the eggs. Break the eggs into a medium-size bowl and add the salt, oregano, and a few grindings of black pepper. Beat the mixture with a table fork for about 30 seconds, or only long enough to combine the ingredients. Stir in the mozzarella cheese and set aside.
Frying the croutons. Pour 4 tablespoons of the olive oil into a 10-inch frying pan with a nonstick surface. Use a pan that can go under the broiler. Set the pan over moderate heat on the range. When the oil begins to appear slightly watery, drop in the bread cubes and, turning them constantly with a spoon, fry them for about 2 minutes, or until they are lightly browned on all sides and have absorbed most of the oil.
Making the omelet and broiling the top. Lower the heat and add the remaining tablespoon of olive oil to the pan. Stir the egg mixture once or twice and pour it into the pan. With a spatula, spread the bread and cheese cubes throughout the eggs as evenly as possible.

Still over low heat, let the omelet cook for 4 to 5 minutes, lifting up an edge with the spatula after 3 minutes or so to see how quickly the underside is browning. Raise or lower the heat if necessary. When the underside is golden brown and the top still somewhat liquid, quickly scatter the Parmesan cheese evenly over the omelet.

Without waiting a second, slide the pan under the preheated broiler and broil the omelet for about 2 minutes, checking it constantly. As soon as the top has puffed and turned a speckled and glistening brown, remove the omelet pan from the broiler.

Serving the omelet. With the spatula, free the edge of the omelet from the pan. Then, firmly grasping the handle of the pan, tilt it at a 45-degree angle and let the omelet slide flat onto a warmed round platter. Serve the omelet at once, or later, at room temperature, cutting it into wedges at the table.

PUFFED CHEESE OMELETS

Although puffy omelets—soufflé omelets to the French—are quite different from scrambled French omelets, they can be filled in a variety of similar ways. The cheese filling described in the following recipe is especially good, but you can use any of the fillings for Filled French Omelets discussed on pages 13–14 (omitting the Tabasco sauce, if desired). And you can, of course, omit the cheese and Tabasco if you prefer a plain puffed omelet.

These omelets should always be made individually, as described below. To make several omelets in succession, just multiply all the listed ingredients, and when you make each omelet, simply pour a heaping cup of the fluffy egg mixture into the pan. If you have two 10-inch nonstick pans and have completely mastered the puffed omelet technique, you can, with some practice, make two omelets simultaneously.

SERVES 1

The Omelet
2 eggs
⅛ teaspoon salt
2 or 3 drops Tabasco sauce
1½ tablespoons butter, cut into bits

The Filling
¼ cup finely shredded natural Cheddar-type cheese, mild or
   sharp

Preparing the eggs. Separate the eggs, dropping the yolks into a small bowl and the whites into a medium-size stainless-steel or glass bowl. Add the salt to the whites and the Tabasco to the yolks.

With a rotary beater, beat the whites rapidly until they form firm, unwavering peaks on the beater when it is lifted upright. Then, using the same beater (no need to wash it), beat the yolks for a few seconds, or only long enough to combine them.

With a rubber spatula, scrape the yolks over the whites and fold the two together, cutting down through the whites and bringing them up and over the yolks, and running the spatula around the sides of the bowl occasionally. Continue folding until only a few streaks of the whites are visible. Be careful not to overfold.
Making the omelet. Working quickly, drop the butter bits into a 10-inch frying pan with a nonstick surface. Set the pan over moderate heat. When the butter has melted but not yet begun to color, tip the pan from side to side to coat the bottom and sides evenly.

With a rubber spatula, scrape the omelet mixture into the center of the pan. Then, using a small metal spatula, quickly spread the omelet so it covers the bottom of the pan without rising up the sides, and make the outer edges of the omelet as round as possible. Reduce the heat to low.

Cook the omelet for about 1 minute to firm the underside, then slide the pan gently back and forth across the burner until the omelet moves freely in one foamy mass. Now let the omelet cook for about 2 minutes more, raising it slightly with the metal spatula after a minute or so to see if the bottom is browning too slowly or too rapidly. If necessary, raise or lower the heat.

In another minute the underside of the omelet should be golden brown and the top should feel warm, not hot, to the touch. The entire cooking time is about 3 minutes.

Immediately remove the pan from the heat and scatter the shredded cheese evenly over the omelet.

Serving the omelet. Without wasting a second, grasp the handle of the pan securely and hold the pan tilted, with its far edge over and just a bit inside the edge of a warmed plate. Insert the metal spatula under the edge of the omelet away from the handle, simultaneously lifting and drawing the pan back until about half the omelet has come to rest on the plate while the other half remains in the pan. Now push the tilted pan forward, using its rim to fold the remaining half of the omelet over as it slides from the pan. This forms a puffed, golden-brown crescent, the cheese enclosed within it. Serve the omelet at once.

VARIATION: SWEET PUFFED OMELETS

Such is the spectacular appearance of a golden, puffy dessert omelet that it can stand quite proudly on its own without being filled at all.

SERVES 1

The Omelet
2 eggs
1 teaspoon granulated sugar
¼ teaspoon vanilla
1½ tablespoons butter, cut into bits

The Topping
Confectioners' sugar

Make these sweet omelets individually, following the techniques described in the preceding recipe. After separating the eggs, add the granulated sugar and vanilla to the yolks, then follow the instructions on pages 19–20.

When the omelet has cooked, and the puffed, golden-brown unfilled crescent is resting on the serving plate, dust its surface with a powdery layer of confectioners' sugar, shaking it out of a canister or sifting it through a fine sieve, before serving it.

VARIATION: PINEAPPLE-FILLED PUFFED OMELETS

You may, if you like, spread a sweet puffed dessert omelet with any jam or jelly or with a fruit filling like the pineapple recipe that follows. Or you can substitute for the pineapple almost any coarsely chopped and drained fresh or canned fruit—apples or peaches, for example. Whatever fruit you use, cook it lightly in butter in precisely the same fashion as the pineapple in this recipe, adding as much sugar as the fruit requires.

SERVES 1

The Filling
2 teaspoons butter, cut into bits
1 teaspoon granulated sugar
¼ cup drained, coarsely chopped canned pineapple, preferably packed in its own juice

The Omelet
2 eggs
1 teaspoon granulated sugar
¼ teaspoon vanilla
1½ tablespoons butter, cut into bits

The Topping
Confectioners' sugar

Preparing the filling. Place the butter bits in an 8-inch nonstick frying pan. Melt the butter slowly over low heat without letting it brown.

Stir in 1 teaspoon granulated sugar, then add the chopped pineapple. Stir continuously over low heat for about 3 minutes, or until the pineapple is thoroughly heated through and covered with a light translucent glaze. If there is any liquid left in the pan, raise the heat to high and, stirring constantly, boil the pineapple for a moment, or until the excess liquid has almost entirely evaporated. Set the filling aside while you prepare the omelet mixture.

Making and serving the omelet. Make each omelet individually, following the techniques described in the recipe for Puffed Cheese Omelets, page 18. After separating the eggs, add 1 teaspoon granulated sugar and the vanilla to the yolks, then follow the remaining instructions.

As soon as the underside of the omelet is golden brown and the top is warm to the touch, remove the pan from the heat and, with a slotted spoon, gently scatter the warm pineapple over the surface of the omelet, leaving behind any juice from the fruit that may have accumulated. Fold the omelet according to instructions, enclosing the pineapple filling within the golden-brown, puffed crescent.

Dust the top of the omelet with confectioners' sugar from a canister or sifted through a fine sieve, and serve the omelets at once.

EGGS IN OTHER GUISES

The "Boiled" Egg

Eggs being the inscrutable objects that they are, "boiling" them demands almost blind faith. In truth, eggs should never be boiled; they should be barely simmered. As simple-minded as it may sound, successful results depend entirely upon precise timing and technique, and good flavor depends upon the age of your eggs. Eggs for soft-boiling should ideally be no more than three days old.

On the other hand, hard-boiled eggs should be at least four or five days old. Even experienced cooks have been baffled by the exasperating phenomenon of finding some hard-cooked eggs easier to peel than others. The reason for this seeming mystery is simply that an older egg has a thinner white that tends to cling less tenaciously to the shell after the egg has been cooked, making older eggs easier to peel than fresher ones.

Another important factor is the temperature of the egg when it enters the boiling water. If the egg was taken directly from the refrigerator, the shell will probably crack as soon as the egg is plunged into the water. To prevent this, let your eggs come to room temperature before cooking them. If you must cook refrigerator-cold eggs, pierce one end of each egg with a needle before placing them in the water. Add 1 minute to the cooking time to compensate for the chill of the eggs.

"SOFT-BOILED" EGGS

5 cups water
4 large eggs, at room temperature and as fresh as possible

Pour the water into a 2-quart saucepan, preferably one of enameled cast iron. Bring it to a boil over moderate heat.

With a long-handled spoon, carefully lower each egg into the water, then cover the pan tightly and turn off the heat. Allow the eggs to remain undisturbed and closely covered for 5 minutes if you like your eggs on the runny side, 6 minutes if you prefer the whites to be somewhat firmer, and 7 minutes if you want them firmer still.

Remove the eggs from the water promptly and serve them immediately, either in eggcups or scooped out with a small spoon into small, preheated custard cups.

"HARD-BOILED" EGGS

5 cups water
4 large eggs, at room temperature and preferably at least 4
    to 5 days old

Pour the water into a 2-quart saucepan, preferably one of enameled cast iron. Bring it to a boil over moderate heat.

With a long-handled spoon, carefully lower each egg into the water, then turn down the heat until the water barely simmers. Let the eggs simmer, uncovered, for exactly 15 minutes.

If you like your hard-cooked eggs hot, serve them as you would the soft-boiled eggs in the preceding recipe.

Hard-cooked eggs to be served cold should be treated in a different manner. After the eggs have cooked their allotted 15 minutes, pour off the hot water and quickly submerge the eggs in cold water. Let them stand in the cold water for 2 or 3 minutes, or until they are cool enough to be handled easily.

To shell the eggs, gently tap each one on a hard surface, rotating it until all of the shell is cracked. Immediately hold the egg under cold running water, and carefully remove the shell and any bits of underlying membrane clinging to the surface. Dry the shelled eggs, let them cool, then wrap them individually in plastic wrap and refrigerate them. They may be safely refrigerated for 2 days or so without discoloring or spoiling.

The Poached Egg

Contrary to popular opinion, poaching an egg is a more predictable process than "boiling" it. The egg, no longer encased in its shell, is in full view, and you will be able to watch and control the cooking.

It is useless to try to poach an egg unless you are certain that it is only one or two days old. As the egg ages (and most supermarket eggs are of more than "a certain age," as the French might say), its white begins to thin; should you attempt to poach such an egg, the white will not cling to the yolk as it should. In fact, the white will separate from the yolk as soon as the egg enters the simmering water, leaving you with, at best, ragged wisps of free-floating egg white and wrinkled, solitary yolks.

Do not add salt to the poaching water; if you do, small pinholes will appear all over the eggs.

Poaching an egg is not to be confused with steaming it, which is what happens to it in a so-called egg poacher. This pan, with its nest of molds, predictably produces neatly shaped rectangular or circular eggs which look as if they had been stamped with a die, their whites almost always overcooked and quite rubbery in texture. An egg "poached" in this fashion need not be particularly fresh; because the white and its yolk are safely contained in their own receptacle, there is no danger of separation.

POACHED EGGS

2 quarts water
2 tablespoons distilled white vinegar
4 large eggs, at room temperature and very fresh

Pour the water into a 10-inch sauté pan (never a black cast-iron pan, which would discolor the eggs); the water should be about 1½ inches deep. If you use another size pan, make sure the water is the required depth. Stir in the vinegar and bring the water to a simmer over moderate heat.

Meanwhile, carefully break each egg into its own custard cup or teacup and spread out 2 or 3 layers of paper towels on which to drain the eggs the moment they are done.

When the water in the pan reaches the simmering point, slide one egg into the water at the side of the pan. Immediately insert a slotted spoon under the egg and carefully turn the white over the yolk two or three times. Then slide each remaining egg into the water, spacing them at wide intervals around the edge of the pan. Be sure to turn each egg repeatedly to envelop it in its white immediately after it enters the water.

Let the eggs simmer for 2 or 3 minutes, or just until the whites are fairly firm and the yolks are still soft. You can test this by gently pressing a yolk with your finger (first dip it in cold water if you are overly sensitive to heat). When the yolk yields only slightly to the touch, the poached egg is done.

Immediately lift each egg out of the water with the slotted spoon, let it drain in the spoon for a moment, then turn the egg out onto the paper towels. Quickly repeat this procedure for each remaining egg. Trim away any ragged edges of the whites, if you wish, with the tip of a small sharp knife.

Serve the eggs at once on hot buttered toast, or use them in any recipe calling for poached eggs.

You may poach eggs up to 10 minutes in advance of serving time by transferring the poached eggs from the simmering water to a small bowl of lukewarm water, where they may rest until you are ready to drain and serve them.

MOCK POACHED EGGS

The French, with their usual ingenuity, long ago discovered a way to cook eggs so that their whites are almost as firm as those of hard-cooked eggs, while their yolks remain soft and fluid. They are called *oeufs mollets,* which means literally, if perhaps inaccurately, soft-boiled eggs; they are more like eggs that are "poached" in their shells. By any name, they make an admirable substitute when you want poached eggs and are unable to find eggs fresh enough to poach in the classic manner.

If you want to cook 8 eggs at a time, just add 1 cup more water (6 cups in all) and follow the recipe below.

    5 cups water
    4 large eggs, at room temperature and preferably about a
        week old
    1-quart bowl of cold water with 6 to 8 ice cubes

Pour the water into a 2-quart saucepan, preferably one of enameled cast iron, and bring it to a simmer over moderate heat.

With a long-handled spoon, carefully lower each egg into the pan and let the eggs simmer for precisely 5 minutes from the time the simmer resumes.

Then, using the spoon, quickly transfer the eggs one at a time to the bowl of iced water, letting them remain there for only 10 to 15 seconds after the last egg has been added.

One at a time, remove the eggs from the water and tap each one gently against a hard surface to make small cracks all over the shell. As carefully as possible, remove all the shell and any bits of membrane that may cling to the fragile surface.

Serve the eggs immediately on hot buttered toast or in individual heated cups; or use them in any recipe calling for poached eggs.

```
┌─────────────────────────────────┐
│          EGGS BENEDICT          │
└─────────────────────────────────┘
```

Perhaps the story is apocryphal, but eggs Benedict are said to have been created by a chef of the old Hotel Waldorf as a restorative for a Mr. Benedict who had imbibed too much the night before. Despite the apparent simplicity of the dish, eggs Benedict require a high degree of organization and timing to complete all the elements at the same time. You can make the sauce, toast the muffins, keep the ham warm, and poach the eggs in any order that works for you.

A serving of two poached eggs Benedict per person makes a substantial luncheon or late-supper dish, but, except for the hollandaise sauce, it is easy enough to cut the recipe in half if you want to serve one egg per person for a late breakfast. Use the leftover hollandaise as a topping for a steak or for hot cooked vegetables, but don't reheat it after it has been refrigerated—the results are unpredictable.

SERVES 4

The Hollandaise Sauce
¼ pound butter, cut into bits
4 egg yolks
2 tablespoons cold butter, cut into bits
¼ teaspoon salt
⅛ teaspoon white pepper
4 teaspoons strained fresh lemon juice
1 to 2 tablespoons heavy cream

The Muffins and Ham
4 English muffins
8 teaspoons butter, softened at room temperature
½ pound sliced boiled ham (2 slices, each about ¼ inch thick), cut into 8 equal squares, at room temperature

The Eggs
8 Poached Eggs, page 26, or Mock Poached Eggs, page 27.

Making the hollandaise sauce by hand. Melt the ¼ pound of butter bits in a small saucepan over low heat, but don't let the butter brown. Set the pan aside.

Pour about 2 or 2½ cups of water into the bottom of a double boiler; be sure it does not touch the bottom of the upper pan. Bring the water to a simmer, then lower the heat.

Meanwhile, off the heat, drop the egg yolks into the upper pan of the double boiler and beat them vigorously with a whisk for about 2 minutes, until they are somewhat thicker than heavy cream. Add 2 tablespoons of cold butter bits to the yolks, together with the salt and white pepper.

Immediately insert the top pan into the base containing the simmering water. With the whisk, beat the yolk mixture for about 2 minutes, until the butter has melted and the mixture has become quite hot and considerably thicker than before. Before you proceed with the next step, it is imperative that the yolk mixture be thick enough to cling to the whisk, yet not so thick that it becomes lumpy or loses all fluidity.

Remove the upper pan from the base and place it nearby, allowing the water in the bottom pan to continue to simmer.

As quickly as possible set the reserved saucepan of melted butter over high heat and reheat it for a few seconds, just until it foams. Then, rapidly stirring the egg mixture—still off the heat—with your whisk, pour in about a teaspoonful of hot butter and whisk for a second or two until it is completely absorbed. Repeat this procedure, teaspoonful by teaspoonful, without ceasing to stir for even a second. When you have added about half the melted butter in this manner, pour in the remaining butter in a slow thin stream, stirring the sauce constantly. Continue to stir for a few more seconds, until the hollandaise is thick, smooth, and glossy. Now stir in the lemon juice, a teaspoonful at a time.

Set the pan into the base containing the simmering water. Whisk the sauce again for about a minute, then stir in 1 tablespoon of the heavy cream. The sauce may now be too thick for your taste; if so, thin it with as much of the remaining tablespoon of cream as you like. Taste the sauce for seasoning and keep it warm in the manner described below.

Making the hollandaise sauce in a blender or food processor. Use the same ingredients listed above, but change the procedure as follows:

Place the egg yolks, salt, pepper, and lemon juice in the container and cover it.

Over high heat melt all the butter—the ¼-pound stick plus the additional 2 tablespoons, all cut into bits—until it foams, but don't let it brown. Remove from the heat. Immediately blend the egg yolk mixture for 4 seconds (at high speed in the blender).

Turn off the machine and scrape down the sides of the container with a narrow rubber spatula. If you are using a blender, replace the cover and blend again for another 4 seconds; this is unnecessary in the food processor.

Without wasting a moment—the butter must be bubbling hot; reheat it if it has cooled too much—turn on the machine (use high speed in the blender) and ever so slowly pour in the butter. Turn off the machine as soon as all the butter has been added. The container will now hold a thick, heavy hollandaise.

Pour the required amount of water into the base of your double boiler and bring it to a simmer.

With a narrow rubber spatula, scrape the hollandaise into the top pan of the double boiler and set it over the simmering water in the base. Stir in 1 tablespoon of the heavy cream, then thin the sauce with as much as you like of the second tablespoon of cream.

Stir the sauce constantly for about a minute to heat it through, then taste it for seasoning. Keep it warm as follows.

Keeping the hollandaise sauce warm. Leave the sauce in the double boiler, but turn off the heat. Stir the sauce briefly every 3 or 4 minutes while you are preparing the other elements in eggs Benedict. Should the sauce become too thick as it rests, thin it with a teaspoonful or more of cream, until it reaches the consistency that you like.

Should the hollandaise sauce curdle, either while you are cooking it or during this resting period, the most satisfactory way to reconstitute it is to whisk about a tablespoonful of boiling water into the sauce and continue to whisk it until the butter and eggs have recombined.

Warming the oven. Heat the oven at the lowest possible setting while you prepare the muffins and ham.

Preparing the muffins and ham. Pierce the English muffins horizontally and closely all around the sides with a table fork, then split them apart gently; don't cut them with a knife, or the cut surface will be flat and the insides will seem doughy. Toast the muffins and spread a teaspoonful of the softened butter over each half.

Arrange two muffin halves on each of 4 individual heatproof serving plates, place a square of ham on each muffin half, and set the plates in the oven to heat the ham and keep the muffins warm.

Poaching the eggs. Poach the eggs according to the instructions or cook and shell Mock Poached Eggs.

Assembling the eggs Benedict. As soon as the eggs are ready, remove the plates from the oven and place an egg on top of each piece of ham. Carefully mask each egg with about 2 tablespoons of hollandaise sauce. Distribute any remaining hollandaise equally over all the eggs and serve at once.

The Shirred Egg

Shirred eggs, called *oeufs miroir* in French, are very much like superbly made fried eggs (which in this country are all too often tough and burned), except that they are broiled instead of fried. They seem to lend themselves to more elaborate treatment than fried eggs. You may sprinkle the cream with a little freshly grated Parmesan cheese before broiling the eggs, or the cream may be omitted altogether, and the eggs merely basted with their butter as they broil.

SHIRRED EGGS

SERVES 4

8 teaspoons butter, softened
8 eggs, at room temperature
Salt
Freshly ground black pepper
¼ cup heavy cream
1 tablespoon chopped fresh parsley, chives, dill, or tarragon
    (optional)

Preheating the broiler. Place the broiling rack so that the ramekins or custard cups will be about 1 inch from the source of heat, and preheat the broiler at its highest setting for 15 minutes.
Precooking the eggs. Place 2 teaspoons of butter into each of 4 shallow ramekins or custard cups about 4 inches in diameter.

Then, one dish at a time, melt the butter over moderate heat but don't let it brown. Drop two eggs into one of the dishes, sprinkle them liberally with salt and a few grindings of pepper, and cook the eggs, undisturbed, for a few seconds until the whites form a thin opaque layer on the bottom of the dish. Put the dish aside while you precook the remaining eggs in the same way (the eggs in this state may wait several minutes before completing the dish).

Finishing and serving the eggs. Just before serving, pour about 2 teaspoons of the cream over the eggs and place the ramekins or custard cups on the broiler rack. Leave the broiler door open and broil the eggs for about 1 minute, using a long-handled spoon or bulb baster to baste them with the cream every 10 seconds until the whites are set and the yolks are still soft. Sprinkle with the fresh herbs, if you wish, and serve at once.

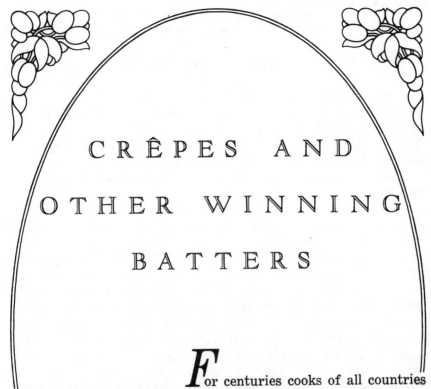

CRÊPES AND OTHER WINNING BATTERS

*F*or centuries cooks of all countries have made their own versions of crêpes, pancakes, and waffles in an array of dishes staggering in their variety. And they serve these dishes not only for breakfast or dessert, as Americans usually do, but as main dishes or accompaniments to other foods for any meal of the day.

As you will see when you explore the recipes in this section, crêpes, pancakes, and waffles can be large or small, thin or puffed, sweet or savory. They can be made substantial by the addition of cheese, shellfish, meats, or fruits, or almost anything else you desire. Yet, despite the obvious differences among these versatile creations, they have more elements in common than you might expect.

For one thing, they are always fried or baked and, with the exception of rectangular waffles, are all circular in shape. They all require manual dexterity, speed in preparation, and coordination—to say nothing of mastering special techniques—if you are to achieve ideal results: the most delicate of crêpes, the tenderest of pancakes, and the crispest of waffles. But even more important, each is made from a batter that is a comparatively simple mixture of flour, liquid, fats, and eggs, and sometimes a leavening agent, usually baking powder and/or baking soda.

Ingredients for Batters

A batter is surely one of the simplest culinary mixtures to prepare, but few cooks know why batters perform as they do or why they sometimes fail to perform as they should.

Flours. Flour is the essential element that gives the batter its body, and the amount and type of flour you use will determine to a great degree the character of your finished crêpes, pancakes, and waffles.

It is crucial to sift and measure flour precisely. Always use dry-measuring (level-measuring) cups. Sift the flour either into the cup itself, mounding it up, or onto a sheet of wax paper, then scoop it lightly into the cup. With the edge of a spatula or the back of a knife, scrape off the surplus flour, leaving a level surface.

Only three recipes in this section require cake flour. All the others specify all-purpose flour. Don't ever substitute cake flour for all-purpose flour, or you are likely to find your crêpes, pancakes, or waffles literally disintegrating before your eyes as they cook. Nor should you use any all-purpose or cake flour that is labeled "self-rising" for these recipes. Such specially prepared flours contain salt and baking powder; obviously, if they are used in recipes calling for additional salt and leavening, the results will be catastrophic.

Liquids. Without the indispensable liquid, a batter, by definition, would be impossible to make. The type of liquid you use will give a batter a definite flavor and texture. This applies particularly to beer and brandy; their alcohol has a tenderizing effect on the mixture.

For the most part, these recipes call for commonplace liquids—water and/or milk; occasionally, they use buttermilk or sour cream.

Leavenings. Of enormous importance to the lightening of certain pancake and waffle batters are leavening agents—baking powder and baking soda, which form the carbon dioxide gas that lightens your pancakes and waffles as they cook. These recipes always specify double-acting baking powder because it releases only a fraction of its carbon dioxide at room temperature after it has been moistened, conveniently reserving the rest for a major thrust when the batter is exposed to heat. It is infinitely preferable to single-acting baking powder, which releases most of its carbon dioxide soon after it has been moistened; batters made with double-acting baking powder can be allowed to rest safely for up to 30 minutes before being cooked.

Baking soda is required in addition to baking powder if you

are to get full leavening action in buttermilk and sour cream batters because it is necessary to take the acid content of those liquids into account. In other words, if you omit the baking soda in these batters, your buttermilk pancakes and sour cream waffles would indeed be as flat as the proverbial pancake and of poor flavor as well.

Fats. Every batter in this section calls for melted fat—at least 2 tablespoons for every cup of batter—and the amount and type of fat you use will have a pronounced effect on the texture and flavor of your finished dishes.

When the recipe calls for butter, unsalted (sweet) butter is preferred. If you must use salted butter, reduce the salt called for in the recipes by about one-half, or to your taste.

Melted vegetable shortening has the same effect as butter on the texture of the batter, but pancakes and waffles made with this comparatively flavorless fat are lacking in the richness only butter can give. Despite this warning, you may substitute melted shortening—or oil, if you wish—for the butter in the recipes for American, buttermilk, and blueberry pancakes and for sour-cream and sweet-cream waffles. But you will be flirting with failure if you use shortening instead of butter in any other recipe in this section.

Another matter altogether is the butter used in cooking crêpes, pancakes, and waffles if you do not have a nonstick pan. Most of these cook so rapidly that the low smoking point of butter is not crucial, and therefore butter alone is used to cook them. However, for those that require longer cooking times, butter is combined with the more heat-resistant vegetable oil (and in one recipe with bacon fat) to raise the smoking point of the fat. Combining fats in this way retains much of the rich flavor of the butter and prevents the otherwise almost inevitable burning.

Eggs. Eggs serve several functions in batters. The most important one is binding the flour, liquid, and other ingredients into a texture far more delicate than that of a batter made without eggs.

Batters in which eggs are separated, with the yolks beaten into the batter first and the stiffly beaten whites folded in just before cooking, will be perceptibly lighter than a batter in which whole eggs are used. The air beaten into the whites acts as additional—or, sometimes, the only—leavening of the mixture.

In addition, eggs, whether separated or whole, have the curious property of expanding or puffing slightly, however briefly, during cooking, and therefore they help to lighten batters.

Finally, because of their distinctive flavor, the contribution of eggs to batters is a qualitative one—eggs give a luxuriousness to crêpes, pancakes, and waffles.

So long as the eggs you use are edibly fresh, they need not be new-laid.

Crêpes: Translated from the French

The words *pancakes* in English and *crêpes* in French have precisely the same meaning; and viewed in their own frames of reference, the English and French versions of pancakes are equally good. But the French, with their expected culinary genius, have managed by some alchemy to transform their pancakes into veritable works of art.

Although crêpes are made from simple batters, as most pancakes are, the French batters are thinner than those typical of other countries and, when properly cooked, are transformed into paper-thin disks.

However, French crêpes can be sturdier on occasion, depending on the dish in which they are to be used. Consequently, this section is divided into two parts: Crêpes for Substantial Dishes, and Dessert Crêpes.

Unlike pancakes, neither type of crêpe is ever served "from pan to plate," as European cooks so succinctly put it. In fact, the crêpes, their fillings, and their sauces may be prepared well in advance. When they are ready to be served, they are filled, rolled, and sauced in a variety of interesting and delicious ways. Once you have mastered the special techniques they require, they will open a culinary world you can explore creatively with confidence and skill—whether you use these recipes or those of your own devising.

Techniques for Making Crêpes

Mixing the batter. Although it is preferable to make crêpe batter by hand, you may mix it in a blender if you wish. The blender-beating process tends to overdevelop the gluten in the flour, which causes the batter to have too much elasticity and produces a tough crêpe. But you can overcome this by allowing the batter to rest for at least an hour before using it: the resting produces a slight relaxation in the gluten structure of a batter, thus ensuring a more tender crêpe.

The rest period is optional for crêpe batter made by hand.

Keeping the batter. Because crêpe batters contain no leavening, they may be kept for a day or two in a tightly covered jar in the refrigerator. The batter will thicken somewhat as it stands. You can bring it back to its original consistency by whisking in a small amount of water when you are ready to use it.

Heating the crêpe pan. Place your crêpe pan over moderate heat for a minute or two, then flick a few drops of cold water into it. If the pan is the correct temperature, the drops will bubble for a second or so before evaporating. If they vanish instantly, your pan is too hot; if they steam away slowly, your pan is not hot enough. Adjust the heat until another few drops of water flicked into the pan behave as they should.

Buttering the crêpe pan. Butter the crêpe pan lightly, whether or not it has a nonstick lining. The butter gives crêpes a richness of taste and an enticing color that they would not otherwise have.

Measuring the batter. With a 2-ounce ladle, a ¼-cup dry-measuring cup, or a large spoon, put a generous quantity of batter in the buttered crêpe pan—about 3 tablespoons for substantial crêpes and 2 tablespoons for dessert crêpes. Tilt the pan from side to side, then pour the excess batter back into the mixing bowl.

Cooking the crêpes. If your pan has been heated to the correct temperature, a thin layer of batter will cling to the bottom of the pan after the excess batter is poured off. Continue to cook the crêpe according to the recipe you are using.

If the crêpe pan has become too hot, the crêpe will curl up and slide back into the bowl when you pour back the surplus batter. Lift the crêpe out of the batter with a fork and discard it. Without returning the pan to the heat, brush it with butter and repeat the crêpe-making procedure with another ladleful of batter. By this time the pan should have cooled to the correct temperature and the crêpe should cling to it.

If the crêpe pan is not hot enough when the batter is poured into it, the batter will not grip its surface. Remove the batter from the pan, butter and heat the pan again, and start over.

The following recipe departs from tradition in that the Crêpes for Substantial Dishes are fried on one side only. This not only simplifies the preparation of the crêpes but, because they will be baked again after they are filled, rolled, and sauced, it results in crêpes that are far more tender than the usual ones that have been fried on both sides.

On the other hand, the Dessert Crêpes are cooked on both sides because they are subjected to only a minimal amount of further cooking after they have been made.

Serving the crêpes. Crêpes will be at their best if they are served on plates that have been warmed, but not heated to the sizzling point. Warm the serving plates in an oven preheated at the lowest possible temperature or in a dishwasher that has a plate-warming setting.

Making crêpes in advance. Crêpes may be made ahead. Once you have cooked the crêpes, let them cool in a stack for about 10 minutes. Then wrap the stack with foil or plastic wrap to prevent the crêpes from drying out. You can leave the wrapped crêpes at room temperature for up to 5 hours or, if they must wait longer, you can refrigerate them for up to 24 hours.

You can also successfully freeze crêpes for up to 4 weeks. In that case, be sure to wrap them securely in aluminum foil or heavy freezer wrap, excluding as much air as possible from the package.

You will have no difficulty at all in separating crêpes if they have been left at room temperature. If they have been refrigerated or frozen, however, let them return to room temperature before attempting to separate them. You can hasten the defrosting process of frozen crêpes by placing the stack of crêpes, closely wrapped in foil, in an oven preheated to 250° F., where they will take 5 to 10 minutes to defrost, depending on the size of the frozen stack. You would be wise to check their progress as they thaw, lest they overheat and become soggy.

You can also prepare any of the filled savory crêpes hours or even a day before you plan to serve them. Simply complete all the steps in the recipe except for baking and browning the filled crêpes. Then cover the dish with plastic wrap or foil and refrigerate it.

Half an hour before you plan to bake the crêpes, remove the baking dish from the refrigerator. At baking time remove the plastic wrap or foil, then follow the recipe precisely for the baking and browning steps.

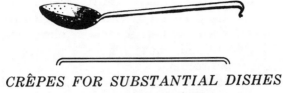

CRÊPES FOR SUBSTANTIAL DISHES

These Crêpes for Substantial Dishes are so named because, when given hearty and savory fillings, they are suitable main courses at dinner. In fact, they need not even be accompanied by vegetables of any kind. They should be served alone in all their glory, with possibly a small bouquet of crisp watercress nestling beside them.

In the dishes that follow the basic recipe for substantial crêpes, you will find not only savory fillings but also a variety of sauces. The substantial crêpes are also used for that Middle European delicacy, cheese blintzes. In these, the crêpes are folded around a filling and are cooked again by frying. The same substantial crêpes appear in totally different guises as the basis of the Mushroom-filled Mound of Crêpes with Sauce Mornay and the Apple-filled Cake of Crêpes (the only dessert in this section), both of which are baked in a stack after filling.

Because Crêpes for Substantial Dishes are subjected to such elaborate treatment after they are cooked, the master recipe calls for a crêpe that is itself free from any dominant flavor. In other words, texture is meant to enclose taste.

MAKES 16 TO 18 CRÊPES, 6 INCHES IN DIAMETER

The Crêpes
¾ cup milk
¾ cup water
3 eggs
1½ cups sifted all-purpose flour
¼ teaspoon salt
3 tablespoons butter, melted but not browned

For Buttering the Pan
2 tablespoons butter, melted but not browned

Making the batter in a blender or food processor. Combine the milk, water, eggs, flour, salt, and 3 tablespoons of melted butter in the blender or food processor container. Cover and blend at high speed for about 10 seconds, or until well blended.

If you are using a blender, with a rubber spatula scrape down the sides of the jar, then cover and blend again at high speed for about 40 seconds more. There is no need for further blending with a food processor.

Pour the batter into a medium-size bowl and cover with plastic wrap.

It is important that the batter rest, unrefrigerated, for an hour before it is used. After this time it should have the consistency of heavy cream. If it is thicker, beat in a teaspoonful of water. If it is still too thick, you may add a second teaspoonful of water, but no more.

Making the batter by hand. In a mixing bowl, combine the ingredients in the same order as for the machine method, and beat them vigorously with a whisk for about 2 minutes. The batter will be fairly smooth, but to make certain that no lumps remain, strain it through a fine-meshed sieve into another bowl, rubbing any tiny lumps through with the back of a spoon.

You may fry the crêpes at once, or you can, if you wish, cover the bowl with plastic wrap and allow the batter to rest for an hour, as described above.

Cooking the crêpes. Over moderate heat, place an 8-inch frying pan with a 6-inch bottom and a nonstick surface. When the pan has reached the proper temperature (as described on page 37), with a pastry brush butter the pan lightly with some of the 2 tablespoons of melted butter.

Using a potholder, quickly lift the pan from the heat and hold it close to the bowl of batter. With a 2-ounce ladle or a ¼-cup dry-measuring cup, dip up about 3 tablespoons of batter and pour it into the pan. Tilt the pan from side to side until the bottom is completely covered. Immediately tip the pan and pour the excess batter back into the bowl, leaving only a thin film of batter clinging to the bottom of the pan. Attached to it will be a small flap or "tongue" created when you tipped the pan to return the excess batter to the bowl.

Return the pan to the heat and cook the crêpe for about a minute, or until the top surface loses its gloss. With a small spatula, loosen the flap, then invert the pan over a large plate. The crêpe will drop out with its cooked side up. Although it may look uneven, don't tamper with the shape of the crêpe or remove the flap.

Brushing the pan with some of the remaining melted butter each time, make the rest of the crêpes exactly as you did the first one, piling them on top of one another, always cooked side up, until all the batter has been used.

Use the crêpes at once in any of the recipes that follow; or store or freeze them as described on page 38.

LOBSTER-FILLED CRÊPES WITH SAUCE MORNAY

MAKES 12; SERVES 4

The Crêpes
12 Crêpes for Substantial Dishes, page 39

The Sauce Mornay
4 tablespoons butter, cut into bits
6 tablespoons flour
2¾ cups milk
½ cup heavy cream
½ teaspoon salt
⅛ teaspoon white pepper
¼ cup grated Switzerland cheese, preferably imported

The Filling
2 tablespoons butter, cut into bits
½ pound cooked lobster, cut into approximately ½-inch pieces; or two 7½-ounce cans of lobster, well drained and cut up (about 2 cups)
1 tablespoon finely cut fresh tarragon, or 1 teaspoon crumbled dried tarragon
¼ teaspoon salt
½ teaspoon dry mustard
1 teaspoon strained fresh lemon juice

The Topping
¼ cup grated Switzerland cheese, preferably imported
1 tablespoon butter, cut into bits

Making the crêpes. Make the crêpes according to the recipe and set them aside while you make the sauce and the filling. Freeze the crêpes you don't use according to the instructions on page 38.
Making the sauce. Place 4 tablespoons of butter bits in a heavy 2-quart saucepan and set the pan over low heat. When the butter has melted but not browned, remove the pan from the heat. Add the flour and stir vigorously with a wooden spoon until the mixture—the roux—is smooth. Then pour over it, all at once, 2 cups of the milk, reserving ¾ cup. With a whisk, beat the roux and milk together until they are fairly well blended.

Return the pan to the stove, this time over high heat, and, whisking constantly, bring the sauce to a boil. When it has become thick and smooth, lower the heat and, stirring frequently, cook the sauce slowly for 2 or 3 minutes to rid it of any floury taste.

Pour 1 cup of the sauce into a medium-size bowl and set it aside to be used later for the lobster filling.

Pour the remaining ¾ cup of milk and the heavy cream into the sauce remaining in the pan. Add ½ teaspoon of salt and the white pepper and whisk until the sauce is smooth. Then stir in ¼ cup of grated Switzerland cheese.

Taste the sauce for seasoning; depending on the saltiness of the cheese, it may well need more salt. Set the pan of sauce aside.
Making the filling. Melt 2 tablespoons of butter bits over moderate heat in a 10-inch frying pan, preferably one with a nonstick surface. When the butter begins to foam, add the lobster pieces. Stir and toss the lobster constantly with a wooden spoon for about 2 minutes, or until it is well coated with the butter and has turned a light pink. Do not let the lobster brown even faintly, or it will toughen.

With a slotted spoon, remove the lobster from the pan, leaving behind any liquid, and drop it into the reserved cup of plain sauce in the bowl. Add the tarragon, ¼ teaspoon of salt, the dry mustard, and the lemon juice. Mix all the ingredients together with a wooden spoon. Taste for seasoning.

You may fill the crêpes immediately, but if you refrigerate the filling for about an hour, it will firm up considerably and be easier to handle.
Assembling the crêpes. On a long sheet of wax paper, lay the crêpes out flat, side by side, browned sides up, and the small flaps facing you.

With a tablespoon, divide the filling equally among the crêpes, placing a mound of filling on the lower third of each crêpe and leaving the flap exposed. Lift up the flap of each crêpe in turn, bring it up over the filling, then gently roll up the crêpe; don't tuck in the sides.

Preheating the oven. Slide an oven shelf into an upper slot and preheat the oven at 375° F. for 15 minutes. If your oven has a separate broiler, preheat it at the same time, first placing the broiling rack about 3 inches from the source of heat.

Saucing the crêpes. Set the pan of sauce over moderate heat and, stirring constantly with a spoon, heat it for 2 or 3 minutes, or until it is lukewarm to the touch.

Pour about ¼ cup of the sauce into a shallow baking-and-serving dish about 13 inches long and 9 inches wide. (Any rectangular or oval baking dish of approximately these dimensions will do; the size needn't be exact.) Tip the dish from side to side so that the sauce spreads and lightly covers the bottom of the dish.

Carefully arrange the crêpes, seams under, down the center of the dish. If they won't all fit crosswise into a single row, place the remaining crêpes lengthwise along the sides of the dish.

With a large spoon, coat the crêpes with the remaining sauce. Don't be concerned if the crêpes aren't completely masked. If you have sauce left over, pour it around the crêpes.

Now scatter ¼ cup of grated Switzerland cheese evenly over the sauced crêpes and dot with the tablespoon of butter bits.

Baking the crêpes. Place the filled dish in the preheated oven and bake the crêpes for about 15 minutes, or until the sauce has barely begun to bubble. Check the crêpes after 10 minutes or so; they may be cooking faster than you think. When the sauce has reached the bubbling point, remove the dish from the oven at once.

Browning and serving the crêpes. If your broiler is in or beneath the main oven compartment, turn it on and preheat it for 5 to 10 minutes, with the broiling pan about 3 inches from the heat. If you have a separate broiler, you will already have preheated it.

Slide the baking dish into the preheated broiler for about 2 minutes, or until the top is a golden crusty brown. Check the crêpes after a minute or so, because the topping burns easily.

Serve the crêpes at once on warmed plates.

CURRIED CRAB-FILLED CRÊPES

MAKES 12; SERVES 4

The Crêpes
12 Crêpes for Substantial Dishes, page 39

The Curry Sauce
4 tablespoons butter, cut into bits
6 tablespoons flour
1 tablespoon curry powder
1 cup homemade or canned chicken broth
1¾ cups milk
½ cup heavy cream
½ teaspoon salt
⅛ teaspoon white pepper
¼ teaspoon strained fresh lemon juice

The Filling
2 tablespoons butter, cut into bits
½ pound fresh crabmeat, or two 6½- or 7½-ounce cans, thoroughly drained, all bits of shell and cartilage removed (about 2 cups)
½ teaspoon salt
⅛ teaspoon white pepper
½ teaspoon strained fresh lemon juice

The Topping
¾ cup heavy cream, chilled
¼ teaspoon salt

Making the crêpes. Make the crêpes according to the recipe and set them aside while you make the sauce and the filling. Freeze the crêpes you don't use, according to the instructions on page 38.
Making the curry sauce. Place 4 tablespoons of butter bits in a heavy 2-quart saucepan and set the pan over low heat. When the butter has melted but not browned, remove the pan from the heat. Add the flour and curry powder and stir with a wooden spoon until the mixture—the roux—is smooth. Then pour in the chicken broth and 1 cup of the milk, reserving ¾ cup. With a whisk beat

the roux and liquid together until they are fairly well combined.

Set the pan over high heat and, whisking constantly, bring the sauce to a boil. When it has become thick and smooth, lower the heat and, stirring frequently, cook the sauce slowly for 2 or 3 minutes to rid it of any floury taste.

Pour 1 cup of the curry sauce into a medium-size mixing bowl and set the bowl aside, to be used later for the crab filling.

Pour the remaining ¾ cup of milk and ½ cup of heavy cream into the sauce left in the pan. Add ½ teaspoon of salt, ⅛ teaspoon of white pepper, and ¼ teaspoon of lemon juice, and whisk until the sauce is smooth.

Taste for seasoning. Depending on the flavor of your curry powder, the sauce may need more salt, pepper, or even more curry powder. If you decide to add more curry, beat it in with a whisk. Set the pan of sauce aside.

Making the filling. Melt 2 tablespoons of butter bits in a 10-inch frying pan, preferably one with a nonstick surface, over moderate heat. When the butter begins to foam, add the crabmeat. Stir the crabmeat constantly with a wooden spoon for about 2 minutes, or until it is well coated with the butter. Do not let it brown even slightly, however, or it will become stringy and tough.

Remove the crabmeat from the pan with a slotted spoon, leaving behind any liquid in the pan, and drop it into the reserved cup of curry sauce in the bowl. Add ½ teaspoon of salt, ⅛ teaspoon of white pepper, and ½ teaspoon of lemon juice, and gently mix all the ingredients together with a wooden spoon. Taste for seasoning; the sauce may need more salt.

You may fill the crêpes immediately, but if you refrigerate the filling for about an hour, it will firm up considerably and be easier to handle.

Assembling the crêpes. On a long sheet of wax paper lay the crêpes out flat, side by side, browned sides up, and the small flaps facing you.

With a tablespoon, divide the filling equally among the crêpes, placing a mound of the filling on the lower third of each crêpe and leaving the flap exposed. Lift up the flap of each crêpe in turn and bring it up over the filling; then gently roll up the crêpe, but don't tuck in the sides.

Preheating the oven. Slide an oven shelf into an upper slot and preheat the oven at 375° F. for 15 minutes. If your oven has a separate broiler, preheat it at the same time, first placing the broiling rack about 3 inches from the source of heat.

Saucing the crêpes. Place the pan of curry sauce over moderate heat and, stirring it constantly with a spoon, heat it for 2 or 3 minutes, or until it is lukewarm to the touch.

Pour about ¼ cup of the sauce into a shallow baking-and-serving dish about 13 inches long and 9 inches wide. (Any rectangular or oval baking dish of approximately these dimensions will do; the size needn't be exact.) Tip the dish from side to side so that the sauce spreads and lightly covers the bottom of the dish.

Carefully arrange the crêpes, seams under, down the center of the dish. If they won't all fit crosswise into a single row, place the remaining crêpes lengthwise at the sides of the dish.

With a large spoon carefully coat the crêpes with the curry sauce. Don't be concerned if the crêpes aren't completely masked, and if you have leftover sauce, pour it between the crêpes.

Baking the crêpes. Place the filled dish in the preheated oven and bake the crêpes for about 15 minutes, or until the sauce has begun to bubble. Check the crêpes after 10 minutes or so; they may be cooking faster than you think. When the sauce has reached the bubbling point, remove the dish from the oven.

Topping, broiling, and serving the crêpes. If your broiler is in or beneath the main oven compartment, turn it on and preheat it for 5 to 10 minutes, with the broiling rack about 3 inches from the heat. If it is a separate broiler, you will already have preheated it.

Quickly pour ¼ cup of chilled heavy cream into a small stainless-steel or glass bowl. Add ¼ teaspoon of salt and, with a whisk or a rotary beater, whip the cream rapidly until it forms slightly wavering peaks on the beater when it is lifted upright over the bowl.

With a rubber spatula, spread the cream over the crêpes; the surface needn't be smooth. Do this very quickly—if you take too long the cream may thin out.

Immediately slide the baking dish into the preheated broiler. Watch it carefully—the top should become golden brown in a minute or less.

Remove the dish from the broiler and serve the crêpes at once on warmed plates.

HERBED SHRIMP-FILLED CRÊPES

MAKES 12; SERVES 4

The Crêpes
12 Crêpes for Substantial Dishes, page 39

The Sauce Crème
4 tablespoons butter, cut into bits
6 tablespoons flour
2½ cups milk
½ cup heavy cream
¾ teaspoon salt
⅛ teaspoon white pepper
¼ teaspoon strained fresh lemon juice

The Filling
1 pound uncooked shrimp
2 tablespoons butter, cut into bits
1 tablespoon chopped shallots or scallions (white part only)
1 tablespoon finely cut fresh dill or 1 teaspoon dried dill weed
¾ teaspoon salt
⅛ teaspoon white pepper
½ teaspoon strained fresh lemon juice

The Topping
1 tablespoon fine dry bread crumbs
1 tablespoon freshly grated Switzerland cheese, preferably
    imported
1 tablespoon butter, cut into bits

Making the crêpes. Make the crêpes according to the recipe and set them aside while you make the sauce and filling. Freeze the crêpes you don't use, according to the instructions on page 38.
Making the sauce. Place 4 tablespoons of butter bits in a heavy 2-quart saucepan and set the pan over low heat. When the butter has melted but not browned, remove the pan from the heat. Add the flour and stir vigorously with a wooden spoon until the mixture—the roux—is smooth. Then pour in 2 cups of the milk, re-

serving ½ cup. With a whisk, beat the milk and roux together until they are fairly well combined.

Set the pan over high heat, and, whisking constantly, bring the sauce to a boil. When it has become thick and smooth, lower the heat and, stirring frequently, cook the sauce slowly for 2 or 3 minutes to rid it of any floury taste.

Pour ¾ cup of the sauce into a medium-size mixing bowl and set it aside to use later in the shrimp filling.

Pour the remaining ½ cup of milk and the heavy cream into the sauce left in the pan. Add ¾ teaspoon of salt, ⅛ teaspoon of white pepper, and ¼ teaspoon of lemon juice, and whisk until the sauce is smooth. Taste it for seasoning; it may need more salt. Set the sauce aside.

Making the filling. Shell the shrimp and, with a small sharp knife, make a shallow incision along the outer curve of each shrimp. With the point of the knife lift out the intestinal vein that runs the length of the shrimp's body about ⅛ inch under the surface. Then cut each shrimp crosswise into approximately ¼-inch pieces. Spread the shrimp on a double thickness of paper toweling and pat them dry with more paper towels.

Over moderate heat melt 2 tablespoons of butter in a 10-inch frying pan, preferably one with a nonstick surface. When the butter begins to foam, add the shallots or scallions and, stirring constantly, fry them for about a minute. Add the shrimp. Still stirring, fry and toss the shrimp for about 2 minutes, or until the pieces are pink and firm. Do not allow the shrimp to brown even slightly, lest they toughen.

Transfer the contents of the frying pan to the reserved sauce in the bowl. Add the dill, ¾ teaspoon of salt, ⅛ teaspoon of white pepper, and ½ teaspoon of lemon juice, and mix all the ingredients gently together with a wooden spoon. Taste for seasoning; the sauce may need more salt.

You may fill the crêpes immediately, but if you refrigerate the filling for about an hour, it will become firmer and easier to handle.

Assembling the crêpes. On a long sheet of wax paper, lay the crêpes out flat, side by side, browned sides up, and the small flaps facing you.

With a tablespoon, divide the filling equally among them, placing a mound of the filling on the lower third of each crêpe and leaving the flap exposed. Lift up the flap of each crêpe in turn, bring it up over the filling, then gently roll up the crêpe; don't tuck in the sides.

Preheating the oven. Slide an oven shelf into an upper slot and preheat the oven at 375° F. for 15 minutes. If your oven has a separate broiler, preheat it at the same time, first placing the broiling rack about 3 inches from the source of heat.

Saucing the crêpes. Place the pan of sauce over moderate heat and, stirring it constantly with a spoon, heat it for 2 or 3 minutes, or until it is lukewarm to the touch.

Pour about ¼ cup of the sauce into a shallow baking-and-serving dish about 13 inches long and 9 inches wide. (Any rectangular or oval baking dish of approximately these dimensions will do; the size needn't be exact.) Tip the dish from side to side so that the sauce spreads and lightly covers the bottom.

Carefully arrange the crêpes, seams under, down the center of the dish. If they won't all fit crosswise into a single row, place the remaining crêpes lengthwise along the sides of the dish.

With a large spoon carefully coat the crêpes with the sauce. Don't be concerned if the crêpes aren't completely masked. If you have sauce left over, you can pour it between the crêpes.

Now scatter the bread crumbs and then the grated Switzerland cheese evenly over the sauced crêpes. Dot with 1 tablespoon of butter bits.

Baking the crêpes. Place the dish in the preheated oven and bake the crêpes for about 15 minutes, or until the sauce has barely begun to bubble. Check the crêpes after 10 minutes or so; they may be cooking faster than you think. When the sauce has reached the bubbling point, remove the dish from the oven.

Browning and serving the crêpes. If your broiler is in or beneath the main oven compartment, turn it on and preheat it for 5 to 10 minutes, with the broiling rack about 3 inches from the heat. If it is a separate broiler, you will already have preheated it.

Slide the baking dish into the preheated broiler for about 2 minutes. Check the crêpes after a minute or so, because the topping burns easily. When the top is a golden, crusty brown, remove the dish from the broiler and serve the crêpes at once on warmed plates.

```
╔══════════════════════════════╗
  CRÊPES WITH SALMON AND
    MUSHROOM FILLING
╚══════════════════════════════╝
```

MAKES 12; SERVES 4

The Crêpes
12 Crêpes for Substantial Dishes, page 39

The Velouté Suprême
4 tablespoons butter, cut into bits
6 tablespoons flour
2 cups homemade or canned chicken broth
2 egg yolks
1 cup heavy cream
¾ teaspoon salt
⅛ teaspoon white pepper
¾ teaspoon strained fresh lemon juice

The Filling
2 tablespoons butter, cut into bits
3 tablespoons finely chopped shallots or scallions
¼ pound mushrooms, finely chopped
4 tablespoons Madeira
2 cups cooked salmon or two 7½-ounce cans, cut into approximately ½-inch pieces
1 tablespoon finely chopped fresh parsley
1 tablespoon finely cut fresh dill or ½ teaspoon dried dill weed

The Topping
¼ cup grated Switzerland cheese, preferably imported, or Parmesan cheese, or a combination of both
1 tablespoon butter, cut into bits

Making the crêpes. Make the crêpes according to the recipe and set them aside while you make the sauce and filling. Freeze the crêpes you don't use, following the instructions on page 38.
Making the sauce. Place 4 tablespoons of butter bits in a heavy 2-quart saucepan and set the pan over low heat. When the butter has melted but not browned, remove the pan from the heat. Add the flour and stir with a wooden spoon until the mixture—the

roux—is smooth. Pour in the chicken broth. With a whisk, beat the roux and broth together until they are fairly well combined.

Set the pan over high heat and, whisking constantly, bring the sauce to a boil. When it has become thick and smooth, lower the heat and, stirring frequently, cook the sauce slowly for 2 or 3 minutes to rid it of any floury taste.

In a small bowl combine the egg yolks with ½ cup of the cream, reserving ½ cup; into this egg-cream mixture stir a few tablespoons of the simmering sauce. Then reverse the process and slowly pour the egg-cream mixture into the saucepan, stirring constantly.

Bring the sauce to a boil and let it boil for about 10 seconds before removing it from the heat.

Add the salt, white pepper, and lemon juice, and whisk until the sauce is smooth. Set the sauce aside.

Making the filling. Melt 2 tablespoons of butter bits in a 10-inch frying pan, preferably one with a nonstick surface, and set the pan over moderate heat. When the butter has melted but not browned, add the chopped shallots or scallions and, stirring continuously with a wooden spoon, cook them for 2 or 3 minutes, until they are translucent but not brown.

Stir in the chopped mushrooms and cover the pan. Let the mixture simmer over moderate heat for about 5 minutes, during which time the mushrooms will have begun to release their moisture. Uncover the pan and, over moderate to high heat and stirring constantly, cook the mushrooms for about 10 minutes, or until the moisture in the pan has evaporated and the mushrooms are dry but not brown.

Pour the Madeira into the pan, raise the heat, and, stirring continuously, cook the wine entirely away.

With a rubber spatula, scrape the mixture—the *duxelles*—into a medium-size mixing bowl. Add the salmon, parsley, dill, and 1 cup of the sauce. With the rubber spatula, gently but thoroughly mix all the ingredients. Taste for seasoning, and add more salt and pepper if you think they are needed.

Assembling the crêpes. On a long sheet of wax paper lay the crêpes out flat, side by side, browned sides up, and the small flaps facing you.

With a tablespoon, divide the filling equally among the crêpes, placing a mound of filling on the lower third of each crêpe and leaving the flap exposed. Lift up the flap of each crêpe in turn, bring it up over the filling, then gently roll up the crêpe; don't tuck in the sides.

Preheating the oven. Slide an oven shelf into an upper slot and preheat the oven at 375° F. for 15 minutes. If your oven has a separate broiler, preheat it at the same time, first placing the broiling rack about 3 inches from the source of heat.

Saucing the crêpes. Thin the remaining sauce with the reserved ½ cup of heavy cream, and set the pan of sauce over moderate heat. Stirring constantly with a spoon, heat it for 2 or 3 minutes, or until it is lukewarm to the touch.

Pour about ¼ cup of the sauce into a shallow baking-and-serving dish about 13 inches long and 9 inches wide. (Any rectangular or oval baking dish of approximately these dimensions will do; the size needn't be exact.) Tip the dish from side to side so that the sauce spreads and lightly covers the bottom of the dish.

Carefully arrange the crêpes, seams under, down the center of the dish. If they won't all fit crosswise into a single row, place the remaining crêpes lengthwise along the sides of the dish.

With a large spoon, coat the crêpes with the remaining sauce. Don't be concerned if the crêpes aren't completely masked. If you have sauce left over, pour it around the crêpes.

Now scatter the grated cheese evenly over the sauced crêpes and dot with the tablespoon of butter bits.

Baking the crêpes. Place the filled dish in the preheated oven and bake the crêpes for about 15 minutes, or until the sauce has barely begun to bubble. Check the crêpes after 10 minutes or so; they may be cooking faster than you think. When the sauce begins to bubble, remove the dish from the oven at once.

Browning and serving the crêpes. If your broiler is in or beneath the main oven compartment, turn it on and preheat it for 5 to 10 minutes, with the broiling pan about 3 inches from the heat. If you have a separate broiler, you will already have preheated it.

Slide the baking dish into the preheated broiler for about 2 minutes, or until the top is a golden crusty brown. Check the crêpes after a minute or so, because the topping burns easily.

Serve the crêpes at once on warmed plates.

VARIATION: CRÊPES WITH CHICKEN AND MUSHROOM FILLING

Follow the preceding recipe, substituting cooked chicken for the cooked salmon, and tarragon (fresh or dried) for the dill.

CRÊPES WITH CHICKEN-LIVER FILLING

MAKES 12; SERVES 4

The Crêpes
12 Crêpes for Substantial Dishes, page 39

The Sauce Suprême
4 tablespoons butter, cut into bits
6 tablespoons flour
1 cup homemade or canned chicken broth
1 cup milk
¾ cup heavy cream
¼ teaspoon salt
⅛ teaspoon white pepper
¼ teaspoon strained fresh lemon juice

The Filling
1 pound chicken livers
2 tablespoons butter, cut into bits
¼ cup finely chopped scallions, including 2 inches of the green tops
2 tablespoons Madeira
2 hard-boiled eggs, page 24, coarsely chopped
¾ teaspoon salt
⅛ teaspoon white pepper

The Topping
2 tablespoons fine dry bread crumbs
1 tablespoon butter, cut into bits

The Garnish
1 tablespoon chopped fresh parsley

Making the crêpes. Make the crêpes according to the recipe and set them aside while you make the sauce and the filling. Freeze the crêpes you don't use, following the instructions on page 38.
Making the sauce. Place 4 tablespoons of butter bits in a heavy 2-quart saucepan and set the pan over low heat. When the butter has melted but not browned, remove the pan from the heat. Add

the flour and stir vigorously with a wooden spoon until the mixture—the roux—is smooth. Then pour in the chicken broth and milk. With a whisk, beat the roux and the liquids together until they are fairly well combined.

Set the pan over high heat, and, whisking constantly, bring the sauce to a boil. When it has become thick and smooth, lower the heat and, stirring frequently, cook it slowly for 2 or 3 minutes to rid it of any floury taste.

Pour ½ cup of the sauce into a medium-size mixing bowl and set it aside for later use in the filling.

Then pour the cream into the sauce remaining in the pan. Add ¼ teaspoon of salt, ⅛ teaspoon of white pepper, and the lemon juice, and whisk until the sauce is smooth. Taste for seasoning; it may need more salt. Set the sauce aside.

Making the filling. Trim away and discard all the fat and any green spots from the chicken livers. Then, with a large knife, dice the livers into approximately ¼-inch pieces. Spread the diced livers out on a double thickness of paper towels and pat them dry with another paper towel.

Melt 2 tablespoons of butter bits over moderate heat in a 10-inch frying pan, preferably one with a nonstick surface. When the butter begins to foam, add the chopped scallions and, stirring constantly with a wooden spoon, fry them for about 2 minutes without letting them brown.

Add the diced chicken livers and, still stirring, fry the mixture for 2 minutes longer, until the livers are lightly browned. Then stir in the Madeira, raise the heat to high, and let the Madeira cook almost entirely away—a matter of a minute or so.

Transfer the contents of the frying pan to the bowl of reserved sauce. Add the chopped hard-boiled eggs, ¾ teaspoon of salt, and ⅛ teaspoon of white pepper and, with a rubber spatula, gently but thoroughly mix all the ingredients.

Taste the filling for seasoning; it may need more salt.

Assembling the crêpes. On a long sheet of wax paper, lay the crêpes out flat, side by side, the browned sides up and the small flaps facing you.

With a large spoon, divide the filling equally among the crêpes, placing a mound on the lower third of each one and leaving the flap exposed. Lift up the flap of each crêpe in turn, bring it up over the filling, and then gently roll up the crêpe; don't tuck in the sides.

Preheating the oven. Slide an oven shelf into an upper slot and preheat the oven at 375° F. for 15 minutes. If your oven has a separate broiler, preheat it at the same time, first placing the broiling rack about 3 inches from the source of heat.

Saucing and topping the crêpes. Place the pan of sauce over moderate heat and, stirring it constantly with a spoon, heat the sauce for 2 or 3 minutes, or until it is lukewarm to the touch.

Pour about ¼ cup of the sauce into a shallow baking-and-serving dish about 13 inches long and 9 inches wide. (Any rectangular or oval baking dish of approximately these dimensions will do; the size needn't be exact.) Tip the dish from side to side so that the sauce spreads and lightly covers the bottom of the dish.

Carefully arrange the crêpes, seams under, down the center of the dish. If they won't all fit into a single row crosswise, place the remaining crêpes lengthwise along the sides of the dish.

With a large spoon, carefully coat the crêpes with the sauce. Don't be concerned if the crêpes aren't completely masked. If you have sauce left over, pour it into the dish between the crêpes.

Now scatter the bread crumbs evenly over the sauced crêpes, then dot the crumbs with 1 tablespoon of butter bits.

Baking the crêpes. Place the filled dish in the preheated oven and bake the crêpes for about 15 minutes, or until the sauce has barely begun to bubble. Check the crêpes after 10 minutes or so; they may be cooking faster than you think. When the sauce begins to bubble, remove the dish from the oven.

Browning and serving the crêpes. If your broiler is in the main oven compartment, turn it on at its highest setting and preheat it for 5 to 10 minutes with the broiling rack about 3 inches from the heat. If you have a separate broiler, you will already have preheated it.

Slide the baking dish into the preheated broiler for about 2 minutes. Check the crêpes after a minute or so, because the topping burns easily. When the top is a golden, crusty brown, remove the dish from the broiler immediately.

Sprinkle the crêpes with the chopped parsley and serve them at once on warmed plates.

CHEESE BLINTZES

Cheese blintzes, a Middle European delicacy, are suitable for any meal of the day, either as a light main course or as a dessert. You may serve them simply sprinkled with confectioners' sugar and cinnamon if you like, but a bowl of sour cream in addition is traditional. There are also those who like their blintzes served with jam, jelly, or preserves in addition to the sour cream.

Blintzes may be fried immediately after they are made, or they can be refrigerated for up to 12 hours, covered with plastic wrap. Remove them from the refrigerator half an hour before you fry them.

MAKES 12; SERVES 4

The Crêpes
12 Crêpes for Substantial Dishes, page 39

The Filling
½ pound creamed cottage cheese
½ pound pot cheese or farmer cheese
2 egg yolks
2 teaspoons sugar
⅛ teaspoon salt
2 egg whites

For Frying
4 tablespoons vegetable oil
4 tablespoons butter, cut into bits

Making the crêpes. Make the crêpes according to the recipe and set them aside while you make the filling. Freeze the crêpes you don't use, following the instructions on page 38.
Making the filling. Place the cottage cheese and the pot or farmer cheese in a fine-meshed sieve set over a medium-size bowl. With a rubber spatula, press the cheese against the bottom and sides of the sieve, forcing it through. Scrape into the bowl any cheese that is clinging to the outside of the sieve.

Drop the egg yolks into the bowl of cheese, add the sugar and salt, and beat the mixture vigorously with a spoon until the ingredients are thoroughly combined.

Taste the mixture; you may want to add more sugar if you prefer a sweeter filling.
Assembling the blintzes. Lay the crêpes out flat, side by side, browned sides up, on a long sheet of wax paper. With a small sharp knife, cut away the flap of each crêpe and trim off any over-browned or brittle edges.

With a large spoon, divide the cheese filling among the crêpes, placing a mound just below the center of each.

With a fork, beat the egg whites for a few seconds, or only long enough for them to reach the frothy stage.

Lift the lower half of each crêpe over the filling so that its edge comes to the center of the crêpe. Dip a pastry brush into the beaten egg whites and lightly coat the exposed sides and upper half of the crêpe. Then fold the sides in toward the center and roll the crêpe forward, thus enclosing the filling securely and making a neat oblong package. Press your finger along the seam of each crêpe to seal it.

Preheating the oven. Preheat the oven at the lowest possible setting. Line a jelly-roll pan with a double thickness of paper towels to drain the blintzes and keep them warm once they have been fried, and place it in the oven, together with the individual serving plates.

Frying the blintzes. Pour 2 tablespoons of the oil into a 12-inch frying pan with a nonstick surface, add 2 tablespoons of the butter bits, and set the pan over high heat. When the butter has melted completely and just begun to foam, lower the heat to moderate.

Carefully place 6 of the blintzes, seams down, in the pan and fry them for about 3 minutes, or until their undersides are golden brown. Peek under one of the blintzes occasionally to make sure it is not browning too rapidly; if necessary, lower the heat. It is absolutely essential that the blintzes be fried gently, not only to heat the filling through, but also to keep them from toughening.

When the undersides are done, turn the blintzes with a wide metal spatula and fry the uncooked side precisely as you did the first side.

Transfer the finished blintzes to the paper-lined pan in the oven to keep warm while you fry the rest.

Add the remaining oil and butter bits to the frying pan and fry the second batch of blintzes in the same fashion, transferring them to the jelly-roll pan to drain the moment they are done.

Serving the blintzes. The blintzes will be at their best if they are served immediately on the warmed plates. If that is impractical, they may remain in the oven for up to 5 minutes after the second batch is done without coming to any serious harm.

MUSHROOM-FILLED MOUND OF CRÊPES WITH SAUCE MORNAY

Crêpes literally rise to new heights in the layered, filled (and often sauced) mounds that the French, with their usual flair for culinary description, call *gateaux,* or cakes. Unlike most cakes, however, these mounds can be either savory or sweet, and the two recipes that follow offer a version of each kind.

Because the mushroom filling for the savory mound is a subtly flavored one, the construction is masked with a Parmesan-flavored sauce instead of a more assertive topping.

To accompany this dish, which is ideal for a substantial luncheon or supper, or even for dinner, serve chilled white wine and a mixed green salad to follow.

SERVES 4

The Crêpes
16 Crêpes for Substantial Dishes, page 39

The Sauce Mornay
4 tablespoons butter, cut into bits
6 tablespoons flour
2 cups milk
1 to 1¼ cups heavy cream
½ teaspoon salt
⅛ teaspoon white pepper
¼ cup finely grated imported Parmesan cheese

The Filling
4 tablespoons butter, cut into bits
½ cup very finely chopped scallions, including 2 inches of the
    green tops
1 pound mushrooms, finely chopped
4 cold hard-boiled eggs, page 24, very finely chopped
2 tablespoons finely grated imported Parmesan cheese
½ teaspoon salt
Freshly ground black pepper
1 tablespoon strained fresh lemon juice

For Buttering the Baking Dish
1 teaspoon butter, softened at room temperature

The Topping
1 tablespoon finely grated imported Parmesan cheese
2 teaspoons butter, cut into bits

The Garnish
Watercress

Making the crêpes. Make the crêpes according to the recipe. With a small sharp knife, cut away the flaps and any irregular edges so that each crêpe is a perfect round. Set the crêpes aside while you prepare the sauce and the mushroom filling.

Making the sauce Mornay. Place 4 tablespoons of butter bits in a heavy 2-quart saucepan and set the pan over low heat. When the butter has melted but not browned, remove the pan from the heat. Add the flour and stir vigorously with a wooden spoon until the mixture—the roux—is smooth. Then all at once pour in the milk. With a whisk, beat the roux and milk together until they are fairly well combined.

Set the pan over high heat, and, whisking constantly, bring the sauce to a boil. When it has become thick and smooth, lower the heat and, stirring frequently, cook the sauce slowly for 2 or 3 minutes to rid it of any floury taste. Remove the pan from the heat.

Pour ½ cup of the sauce into a small bowl and set it aside for later use in the filling.

With a whisk, stir the sauce remaining in the pan while you slowly pour in 1 cup of the heavy cream, reserving ¼ cup. When the cream is completely absorbed, stir in ½ teaspoon of salt, ⅛ teaspoon of white pepper, and ¼ cup of grated Parmesan cheese. Taste the sauce Mornay for seasoning and set it aside.

Making the filling. Place 4 tablespoons of butter bits in an 8- or 10-inch frying pan, preferably one with a nonstick surface, and set the pan over moderate heat. When the butter has melted but not browned, add the chopped scallions. Stirring continuously with a wooden spoon, cook them for 2 or 3 minutes, or until they are translucent but not brown.

Stir in the chopped mushrooms and cover the pan. Let the mixture simmer over moderate heat for about 5 minutes, during which time the mushrooms will have begun to release their moisture. Uncover the pan and, over moderate to high heat and stirring almost constantly, cook the mushrooms for about 10 minutes, or until the moisture in the pan has evaporated.

With a rubber spatula, scrape the mixture into a medium-size mixing bowl. Add the chopped eggs, 2 tablespoons of grated Parmesan cheese, ½ teaspoon of salt, a liberal grinding of black pepper, and the lemon juice. With your wooden spoon, stir the ingredients together until they are thoroughly combined.

One tablespoonful at a time, stir the reserved plain sauce into the mushroom-and-egg filling. Taste for seasoning, and add more salt and pepper if you think it necessary.

Assembling the mound. With a pastry brush spread 1 teaspoon of softened butter on the bottom of a 9-inch ovenproof glass pie plate. (If you prefer, use a baking-and-serving dish of enameled cast iron or tin-lined copper that is approximately the same size.)

Lay one of the crêpes, cooked side down, in the dish. With a rubber spatula, spread a little less than 2 tablespoons of the filling over the crêpe, then place another crêpe on top, cooked side down. Spread a similar amount of filling over the second crêpe and repeat the procedure with the remaining crêpes and filling, topping the mound with the last crêpe, cooked side up.

Pour ½ cup of the completed sauce Mornay over the mound, letting the excess drip down the sides. Then, with a rubber spatula, spread the excess sauce around the sides, as if you were frosting a cake. Reserve the remaining sauce Mornay.

If the mound at this point seems the slightest bit lopsided, reshape it gently with your spatula.

Sprinkle the top with 1 tablespoon of grated Parmesan cheese and dot it evenly with 2 teaspoons of butter bits.

At this point you may, if you wish, cover the mound with plastic wrap and refrigerate it for up to 6 hours before baking it. In that event, cover and refrigerate the remaining sauce as well.

Preheating the oven. Slide an oven shelf into an upper slot and preheat the oven at 375° F. for 15 minutes.

Baking the mound of crêpes and heating the sauce Mornay. Place the baking dish in the preheated oven and bake for 15 to 25 minutes, or until the top of the mound is delicately browned.

Two or 3 minutes before the mound of crêpes is done, bring the sauce almost to a boil over moderate heat, stirring it constantly with a whisk. If the sauce seems too thick for your taste, whisk in as much of the remaining ¼ cup of heavy cream as you like. Pour the sauce into a serving bowl.

Serving the mound of crêpes. Surround the mound of crêpes as fancifully as you like with sprigs of watercress. Serve it from the baking dish, cutting the mound into wedges as you would a cake, and passing the bowl of sauce Mornay.

AN APPLE-FILLED CAKE OF CRÊPES

For this dessert, seek a brand of canned or bottled applesauce of really good flavor—not always an easy matter. Failing that, you may wish to make the applesauce yourself, if you are fortunate enough to have a source of good cooking apples.

Not the least of the charms of this fruit-filled mound of crêpes is its ability to withstand refrigeration for as long as six hours before it is baked and served with its accompaniment of whipped cream. Since it is a fairly substantial dessert, it utilizes the sturdy Crêpes for Substantial Dishes, which function as thin cake layers, rather than the more delicate dessert crêpes.

SERVES 4 TO 6

The Crêpes
16 Crêpes for Substantial Dishes, page 39

The Filling
3 cups applesauce (about two 15-ounce jars)
2 tablespoons granulated sugar
2 tablespoons butter, cut into bits
½ cup coarsely chopped unsalted pistachio nuts or slivered toasted almonds

For Buttering the Dish
1 tablespoon butter, softened at room temperature

The Topping
2 tablespoons butter, melted but not browned
1 tablespoon granulated sugar

The Whipped Cream
1 cup chilled heavy cream
2 teaspoons confectioners' sugar
1 teaspoon vanilla

Making the crêpes. Make the crêpes according to the recipe. With a small sharp knife, cut away any irregular edges and the flaps so that each crêpe is perfectly round. Set the crêpes aside while you make the filling.

Making the filling. Pour the applesauce into a 12-inch frying pan with a nonstick surface. Set the pan over high heat and bring the applesauce to a boil. Stirring almost constantly, boil the applesauce rapidly, uncovered, for 6 to 8 minutes, or until it has reduced to about 2 cups. Don't be too concerned if there is a little less or a little more than 2 cups; it is more important that the applesauce be thick enough to hold its shape almost solidly when lifted up in a spoon.

Lower the heat and add 2 tablespoons of granulated sugar and 2 tablespoons of butter bits, and stir until the sugar and butter are dissolved in the applesauce. Remove the pan from the heat.

Taste for sweetness; depending on the applesauce, you may wish to add more sugar. Set the filling aside.

Assembling the cake. With a pastry brush, spread 1 tablespoon of softened butter on the bottom of a 9-inch ovenproof glass pie plate. (If you prefer, use an enameled cast-iron or tin-lined copper baking-and-serving dish of approximately the same size.)

Lay one of the crêpes, cooked side down, in the baking dish. With a rubber spatula, spread 2 tablespoons of the filling over the crêpe, then sprinkle about a teaspoonful of the chopped nuts over the top. Place another crêpe over the filling, cooked side down, and repeat the layering of crêpes, applesauce, and nuts, finishing the stack with the last crêpe, cooked side up.

If the cake seems the slightest bit lopsided, gently pat it into shape with your hands or a rubber spatula.

At this point you may, if you wish, cover the cake with plastic wrap and refrigerate it for up to 6 hours before baking it. It should be removed from the refrigerator 30 minutes before baking time.

Preheating the oven. Slide an oven shelf into an upper slot and preheat the oven at 375° F. for 15 minutes.

Baking the cake. Pour 2 tablespoons of melted butter over the top of the cake, then sprinkle it as evenly as possible with the tablespoon of granulated sugar.

Bake the cake in the preheated oven for 20 to 25 minutes, or until it has puffed ever so slightly and the top is golden brown.

Whipping the cream. While the cake is baking, pour the heavy cream into a chilled medium-size glass or stainless-steel bowl. With a large whisk or rotary beater, beat the cream vigorously until it thickens slightly. Then add the confectioners' sugar and vanilla and continue to beat the cream only until it forms soft wavering peaks when the beater is lifted upright over the bowl.

Pile the cream lightly into a serving dish.

Serving the cake of crêpes. Serve the cake while it is still warm, cutting it into wedges at the table. Pass the bowl of whipped cream.

DESSERT CRÊPES

The batter for dessert crêpes, unlike that for the substantial crêpes on page 39, is a flavored one, and it produces a pancake of a far more delicate texture. For the most part, the French do little more with these paper-thin crêpes than wrap them around fragile fruits or sauce them with liqueur-flavored butters, flaming them with Cognac more often than not.

What distinguishes a well-made dessert crêpe from one that is poorly made is its thinness and delicacy, achieved by the rapidity with which it has been cooked. Even experienced cooks have difficulty making a crêpe in the orthodox fashion—that is, by cooking it on one side, then turning it over with a spatula to cook the other side. The crêpe is so delicate that unless you use your fingers, it is almost impossible to carry out this precarious maneuver without tearing it.

To circumvent this hazard, as well as to enable you to make many crêpes speedily, the following method, which is admittedly unorthodox, uses a technique that employs two pans instead of one. Once you have mastered the procedure, you will discover yourself turning out crêpe after crêpe as if to the beat of a metronome. You can, of course, use the one-pan method if you like, but you will find that making the crêpes in two pans will not only save you precious time but give you superior results.

MAKES 16 TO 18 CRÊPES 5 INCHES IN DIAMETER

The Crêpes
¾ cup milk
⅓ cup water
1 cup sifted all-purpose flour
⅛ teaspoon salt
1 egg
2 egg yolks
2 teaspoons sugar
2 tablespoons Cognac, or any good imported or domestic
   brandy
4 tablespoons butter, melted but not browned

For Buttering the Pan
2 tablespoons butter, softened at room temperature or melted

Making the batter in a blender or food processor. Combine the milk, water, flour, salt, egg, egg yolks, sugar, Cognac or brandy, and 4 tablespoons of melted butter in the blender or food processor container. Cover and process at high speed for about 10 seconds, or until well blended.

If you are using a blender, with a rubber spatula scrape down the sides of the jar, then cover and blend again at high speed for about 40 seconds more. There is no need for further blending with a food processor.

Pour the batter into a medium-size bowl, cover with plastic wrap, and set aside. It is important that the batter rest, unrefrigerated, for an hour before it is used. After this time it should have the consistency of heavy cream. If it is thicker, stir into it a teaspoonful of water. If it is still too thick, you may add a second teaspoonful of water but no more.

Making the batter by hand. In a mixing bowl, combine the ingredients in the same order as for the machine method, and beat them together vigorously with a whisk for about 2 minutes. The batter will be fairly smooth, but to make certain that no lumps remain, strain it through a fine-meshed sieve into another bowl, rubbing any tiny lumps through with the back of a spoon.

You may fry the crêpes at once; or you may, if you wish, allow the batter to rest as described above.

Cooking the crêpes. Place a 6½-inch cast-iron crêpe pan with a 5-inch bottom over moderate heat on one burner, and on an adjoining burner, over low heat, place an 8-inch frying pan with a

6-inch bottom and a nonstick surface. Test the heat of both pans, following the directions on page 37.

With a pastry brush, lightly butter the crêpe pan with a little of the 2 tablespoons of softened or melted butter. Do not butter the frying pan.

Using a potholder, lift the buttered crêpe pan from the heat and hold it close to the bowl of batter. With a 2-ounce ladle or a large spoon, ladle about 2 tablespoons of batter into the pan. Tip the pan from side to side until the bottom is completely covered with batter, then immediately tilt the pan and pour the excess batter back into the bowl. Only a thin film of batter should cling to the bottom of the pan; attached to it will be a small flap or "tongue" (created by tilting the pan to return the excess batter to the bowl) which you should leave intact.

Return the pan to moderate heat and cook the crêpe for about a minute, or until the top loses its gloss and the edges show the faintest rim of gold.

With a small spatula, loosen the flap, then invert the crêpe over the 8-inch frying pan. The crêpe will fall out easily, browned side up. Let it fry for about 30 seconds, then lift the pan, hold it at a slight angle, and let the crêpe slide out onto a large plate. The second side will be speckled rather than brown, and will become the inside of the dessert crêpe.

Brushing the crêpe pan with some of the remaining softened or melted butter each time, make the rest of the crêpes exactly as you did the first one, stacking them on top of one another until all the batter has been used.

Use the crêpes at once in any of the following recipes, or store or freeze them as described on page 38.

FLAMBÉED CRÊPES WITH ORANGE BUTTER SAUCE

This is a version of the classic crêpes suzette. It differs from the original insofar as it is far easier to prepare and doesn't require a formidably expensive crêpes suzette pan and table burner.

Moreover, you need not carry through the entire operation without interruption from start to finish. You can make the crêpes ahead of time as described on page 38, then complete the orange butter sauce and refrigerate it. When you are ready to present the dessert, simply sauce and flame the crêpes in the kitchen and serve them promptly on warmed plates, following the directions below.

MAKES 16; SERVES 4

The Crêpes
16 Dessert Crêpes, page 63

The Orange Butter
8 tablespoons butter (a ¼-pound stick), softened at room temperature
4 tablespoons sugar
3 tablespoons strained fresh orange juice
1 tablespoon orange liqueur (Grand Marnier, Curaçao, or Triple Sec)
1 tablespoon very finely chopped orange peel

For Topping and Flaming
2 tablespoons sugar
¼ cup Cognac, or any good imported or domestic brandy

Making the crêpes. Make the crêpes according to the recipe. With a small sharp knife, cut away the flap on each crêpe. Set the crêpes aside while you prepare the orange butter.
Preparing the orange butter. With a wooden spoon, cream the butter, mashing and rubbing it against the sides of a large heavy bowl. Then add 4 tablespoons of sugar and beat vigorously until the mixture is smooth and fluffy. Beat in the orange juice about a teaspoonful at a time, beating well after each addition. When all

the juice has been absorbed, beat in the orange-flavored liqueur, then stir in the finely chopped orange peel. Set the bowl aside.

Warming the dishes and assembling the ingredients. Heat your oven at the lowest possible temperature and in it warm a shallow baking-and-serving dish about 8 or 9 inches in diameter and the dessert plates.

On a long sheet of wax paper, lay the crêpes out flat, side by side, speckled sides up. Set the heated baking dish close at hand, together with the bowl of orange butter.

Saucing the crêpes. Place about 2 tablespoons of the orange butter in a 10-inch frying pan, preferably one with a nonstick surface. Set the pan over moderate heat.

When the butter has melted and begun to froth—don't let it brown even slightly—add a crêpe to the pan, laying it flat with its speckled side up. With a long-handled spoon, baste the crêpe thoroughly with the hot flavored butter. When it is completely coated, secure it at one side with a fork, and with your spoon fold it in half, then fold it in half again to form a quarter-circle. Transfer the crêpe to the heated baking dish.

In precisely the same fashion, baste and fold the remaining crêpes, adding a teaspoonful or more of orange butter to the pan after every crêpe or two, and regulating the heat to prevent any browning. The pan should always contain enough butter to baste each crêpe thoroughly.

As you place the folded crêpes in the baking dish, lay them around the edge, overlapping them slightly. When the sides of the dish are completely lined, place the remaining crêpes in the center. Then immediately sprinkle the crêpes evenly with 2 tablespoons of sugar.

Flaming the crêpes. Pour the Cognac into the smallest saucepan you have and place it over low heat. Let the Cognac warm for a few seconds, only long enough for it to become tepid. Then, stepping back, set it alight with a kitchen match.

Slowly pour the flaming Cognac evenly over the crêpes and, with the long-handled spoon, baste the crêpes rapidly with the flaming sauce.

When the sauce stops flaming, arrange 4 crêpes on each warmed dessert plate. Moisten each crêpe with the sauce remaining in the pan and serve at once.

DESSERT CRÊPES WITH BANANA AND APRICOT FILLING

MAKES 12; SERVES 4

The Crêpes
12 Dessert Crêpes, page 63

The Filling
3 tablespoons apricot jam
6 ripe but firm bananas, each about 6 inches long
1 teaspoon strained fresh lemon juice

For Buttering the Dish
1 tablespoon butter, softened at room temperature

The Topping
2 tablespoons butter, softened at room temperature
1 to 2 tablespoons sugar

Making the crêpes. Make the crêpes according to the recipe and set them aside while you make the filling. Freeze any crêpes you don't use, according to the instructions on page 38.

Preparing the filling. In a small bowl, beat the apricot jam with a small wooden spoon until it is as smooth and fluid as possible.

Peel the bananas and, with a small sharp knife, cut off and discard about an inch from each end. Then cut the bananas in half lengthwise. You will have 12 pieces, each about 4 inches long. To prevent the bananas from discoloring, place them in a glass or stainless-steel bowl and, using a wooden spoon, roll them gently in the lemon juice.

Preheating the oven. Slide an oven shelf into an upper slot and preheat the oven at 375° F. for 15 minutes.

Assembling the crêpes. With a pastry brush, spread 1 tablespoon of softened butter on the bottom of a shallow baking-and-serving dish about 9 inches wide and 13 inches long. (Any rectangular or oval dish of these approximate dimensions will do.)

On a long sheet of wax paper lay the crêpes out flat, side by side, speckled sides up and with the flaps facing you. With your pastry brush, gently spread the entire exposed surface of each crêpe with apricot jam, taking care not to tear the delicate crêpes. Then lay a piece of banana, cut side down, on the lower third of each crêpe and carefully roll up the crêpe, enclosing the banana; don't tuck in the sides.

As each crêpe is rolled, place it, seam side down, in the buttered baking dish, leaving at least ¼ inch between them.

With a clean pastry brush, coat the crêpes with 2 tablespoons of softened butter, then sprinkle them lightly with as much of the sugar as you like.

Baking and serving the crêpes. Place the baking dish in the preheated oven and bake the crêpes for about 12 minutes, or until the tops are golden and the edges crisp. To be on the safe side, check the crêpes after they have baked for 10 minutes; they may very well be done by that time.

Serve the crêpes at once directly from the baking dish on warmed plates.

VARIATION: PINEAPPLE-FILLED DESSERT CRÊPES

The Filling
1 can (20 ounces) crushed pineapple packed in syrup
2 tablespoons butter, softened at room temperature

Follow the preceding recipe, substituting the pineapple for the banana-apricot filling. To make the filling, drain the crushed pineapple in a sieve set over a bowl and reserve the syrup. Dry the pineapple out on a double thickness of paper towels, then transfer the pineapple to a bowl. You should have about 1½ cups.

Measure ¾ cup of the reserved pineapple syrup and pour it into a 10-inch frying pan, preferably one with a nonstick surface. Set the pan over high heat, bring the syrup to a boil, and let it boil briskly, uncovered, for 5 minutes or so, or until it has thickened and reduced to about ½ cup.

Remove the pan from the heat, stir in 2 tablespoons of softened butter, and set the pan of syrup aside while you assemble the crêpes.

With your pastry brush, gently spread each crêpe with the pineapple syrup. Then divide the 1½ cups of drained pineapple equally among the crêpes, placing a mound on the lower third of each one, and leaving the flap exposed. Carefully roll up each crêpe, but don't tuck in the sides.

Pancakes: Plain and Fancy

An exploration of the evolution of pancakes would have to start in China, wend through every past civilization of the world, dwell for a while in such illustrious pancake-making countries as France, Sweden, Norway, Finland, and Russia, among others, and finally come to rest in the United States, where the tour would end not with a bang but a whimper. Here the result of this glorious heritage is pancake restaurants by the hundreds and box after box of pancake mixes lining our supermarket shelves. Not that they are all that bad, but too many of us seem to have forgotten how remarkably good honestly made pancakes can be.

In the following pages are recipes for a variety of generic pancake batters that are representative of several countries in addition to our own. Most pancake batters, apart from those leavened with yeast, are essentially similar. But it will interest you to note the variations among them.

Some of the batters in this section contain very little flour, others none at all—the German Potato Pancakes include a trifling amount, whereas the Crispy Potato Pancakes, which are somewhat different in texture and flavor, contain none. The creamy Cottage-Cheese Pancakes contain only enough flour to bind the eggs and cheese delicately together. With exceptions such as these, the batters are basically the same, although the incredible number of guises they assume might lead you to suspect otherwise.

Techniques for Making Pancakes

Mixing the batter. All pancake batters should be mixed by hand. It takes very little effort and the results are infinitely preferable to pancakes from batters made by mechanical means. Mixing the batter in a blender or food processor—in fact, overmixing it by hand—will overdevelop the gluten and thus toughen the pancakes. Moreover, a machine is apt to liquefy or homogenize solid ingredients such as those in the potato, cottage-cheese, and spinach pancakes.

Keeping the batter. Almost all the following pancake batters are at their best when used immediately. However, you can allow batters made with double-acting baking powder to stand for up to 30 minutes without any noticeable ill effects. This does not apply to batters that include beaten egg whites; such batters are best cooked at once.

Heating the pan or griddle. Place the range-top griddle or frying pan over moderate heat, or preheat the electric griddle or frying pan at 400° F. But before you begin to cook your pancakes, test the heat by flicking a few drops of cold water onto the hot surface. The drops should bubble in a lively fashion for a second or two before evaporating. If they skitter and dance off the surface instantly, your griddle is too hot; if they steam and evaporate slowly, the surface is too cool. Raise or lower the heat as needed until another few drops of water flicked onto the surface behave as they should.

Buttering the griddle or frying pan. You will note that the recipes call for buttering the griddle or frying pan lightly for some pancakes and more heavily for others. This applies to all griddles and frying pans, whether they have a nonstick lining or not. The butter gives pancakes a richness of taste and an enticing color that they would otherwise lack.

Measuring the batter. The recipes that follow show a decided preference for pancakes that are small rather than large. You can, however, make the pancakes any size you like. Use a 2-ounce ladle, a dry-measuring cup, or a large spoon and measure into it the specified amount of batter. Mark this level with your eye, and as you make your pancakes, fill it with batter to the same level each time.

With experience, some cooks can pour almost any batter directly onto the griddle or frying pan without measuring, but if you are a novice cook, you would be safer to follow the directions for measuring precisely.

Cooking the pancakes. When the griddle is the correct temperature, quickly fill it with batter for pancakes, leaving at least one inch or more between them so you can turn each pancake easily. Then cook them according to the recipe.

If your pancakes are made with leavening agents, don't peek at the underside to see how fast they are cooking. If you disturb leavened pancakes before the first side is really done, the premature peeking may prevent them from rising to their maximum lightness. On the other hand, it is good culinary practice to lift the edge to check the browning of unleavened pancakes—the potato and spinach pancakes, for example.

Do not be tempted to turn any pancake more than once. This is especially true for leavened pancakes. A second turning will inevitably toughen them. If you bake the pancakes as directed and turn them at the proper moment, they will be perfectly cooked throughout.

Sooner or later, you will notice that the second side of some pancakes—American, buttermilk, blueberry, for example—are speckled and never as evenly browned as the first side. This curious phenomenon is the result of the action of sugar in the batter, which tends to caramelize on the first side of the pancake that is exposed to heat. You can turn this phenomenon to decorative effect: Just before turning the pancake, make a design on the uncooked side with a small stream of granulated sugar. As a result, you will have a finished pancake with your own design etched in caramelized sugar. Needless to say, serve these pancakes with the design side up.

Serving the pancakes. Ideally, all pancakes should go directly from the griddle or pan to warmed serving plates because they are at their best the moment they are done. Moreover, because pancakes are small, they tend to cool very rapidly if served on cold plates. While cooking pancakes, warm the serving plates in an oven that has been preheated at the lowest possible temperature, or in a dishwasher that has a plate-warming setting.

Some of the pancakes in this section can wait for a few minutes if they are kept warm in the oven. These are indicated in the individual recipes.

AMERICAN PANCAKES

However traditional it may be, the American practice of stacking pancakes and separating them by pats of butter is an unfortunate one. Not only do the pancakes become soggy because of the steam trapped between them, but the butter usually melts into an unattractive puddle in the center of each pancake.

It is a further affront to these light pancakes to pour syrup over the stack. Instead, arrange them in a circle on each plate, 3 or 4 pancakes to a serving, overlapping the edges of the pancakes slightly if your plates are small. Serve the pancakes with melted butter and any of the following accompaniments:

Melted butter. A bowl of hot, but not browned, butter, preferably unsalted, is a must. A quarter-pound stick should be sufficient for 4 servings of pancakes.

Pure maple syrup. Although expensive, maple syrup is certainly preferable to so-called pancake syrup, in which comparatively small amounts of maple syrup are mixed with cane, corn, or other syrups. Whatever syrup you use, heat it to lukewarm and present it in a pitcher, or in a bowl with a ladle.

Honey. Honey is delightful in place of maple syrup. Experiment with the many varieties available in supermarkets today. Again, as with maple syrup, serve it from a bowl; and if it seems too thick for your taste, heat it just to lukewarm in the top of a double boiler over barely simmering water.

Honey-butter cream. This silky, sweet cream is easily made by beating about ¼ cup of honey into a quarter-pound of softened butter. Mound it in a bowl for serving.

MAKES ABOUT 16; SERVES 4

The Batter
1½ cups sifted all-purpose flour
2 teaspoons double-acting baking powder
½ teaspoon salt
1½ tablespoons sugar
2 egg yolks
1 cup milk
¼ cup water
4 tablespoons butter, melted but not browned
2 egg whites

For Buttering the Griddle
2 tablespoons butter, softened at room temperature

Preparing the batter. In a small bowl combine the flour, baking powder, salt, and sugar. Stir lightly with a fork and set aside.

Drop the egg yolks into a large mixing bowl and pour in the milk, the water, and the melted butter. Using a whisk or a fork, beat them together for 8 to 10 seconds, or just until they are mixed.

Hold a sifter over the large mixing bowl, then pour in the

flour mixture and sift it into the bowl. With a fork—not a whisk —stir the dry and liquid ingredients together, running the back of the fork around the sides of the bowl from time to time to dislodge any clinging flour. After a moment or so of stirring, the pancake batter should be quite fluid but slightly lumpy. Do not overmix it or attempt to rid the batter of any small lumps.

Preheating the griddle. Before completing the batter, preheat an electric or built-in range griddle to 400° F. or set a range-top griddle over moderate heat.

Because it is important that you work quickly when you begin cooking the pancakes, place the softened butter, a pastry brush, and a wide metal spatula close at hand.

Completing the batter. With a rotary beater, beat the egg whites in a small glass or stainless-steel bowl until they form firm peaks on the beater when it is lifted. With a rubber spatula, immediately scrape the whites over the batter and fold them in. Cut down through the mixture with the spatula and lift the heavier batter over the whites, occasionally running the spatula across the bottom and around the sides of the bowl. Continue the folding process just until no streaks of egg white show. Be careful not to overfold, or you will lose the air you have beaten into the egg whites.

The batter will be rather thick but fluid. Pour it immediately into a quart-size glass measuring cup or a pitcher.

Cooking the pancakes. Test the heat of your griddle as described on page 71. Then, with the pastry brush, lightly coat the surface with some of the softened butter.

Holding the spout of the measuring cup or pitcher about an inch above the griddle, pour enough batter in a slow stream to spread out and form a pancake about 4 inches in diameter. Working quickly, fill the griddle, using the same amount of batter for each pancake and leaving at least an inch between them.

In a minute or two, tiny pinholes will appear on each pancake; a moment or so later a few small bubbles will rise. As soon as two or three of the bubbles in the first pancake burst, slide the metal spatula under it and turn it over. At the proper moment turn each of the remaining pancakes. Bake the second side about half as long as the first.

Strongly resist any temptation to peek at the undersides as the pancakes bake, and do not turn the cakes more than once. If you feel, after baking the first batch, that the second batch would be improved by increasing or decreasing the baking time, make the proper adjustment the second time around.

Serving the pancakes. As soon as each batch of pancakes is done, serve at once on heated plates, together with melted butter and any of the other accompaniments suggested in the introduction to this recipe.

BUTTERMILK PANCAKES

MAKES ABOUT 16; SERVES 4

The Batter
2 cups sifted cake flour
2 teaspoons double-acting baking powder
1 teaspoon baking soda
2 tablespoons sugar
1 teaspoon salt
2 eggs
1½ cups buttermilk
3 tablespoons butter, melted but not browned

For Buttering the Griddle
2 tablespoons butter, softened at room temperature

Preparing the batter. In a small bowl, combine the cake flour, baking powder, baking soda, sugar, and salt. Stir together lightly with a fork and set aside.

Break the eggs into a large mixing bowl and pour in the buttermilk and melted butter. With a fork, beat them together for 8 to 10 seconds, or only until well combined.

Hold a sifter over the large mixing bowl, then pour in the flour mixture and sift it into the bowl. With the fork, stir the dry and liquid ingredients together, running the back of the fork around the sides of the bowl from time to time to dislodge any clinging flour. After a moment or so of stirring, the pancake batter should be fairly smooth and quite thick. Don't overmix it; a few small lumps will do no harm.

Ideally, the batter should be used immediately, but if it must wait, set it aside, unrefrigerated and covered with plastic wrap, for no longer than 30 minutes.

Preheating the griddle. Preheat an electric or built-in range griddle to 400° F., or set a range-top griddle over moderate heat.

Because it is important that you work quickly when you start cooking the pancakes, place the softened butter, a pastry brush, a wide metal spatula, and a 2-ounce ladle or a ¼-cup dry-measuring cup close at hand.

Cooking the pancakes. Test the heat of your griddle as described on page 71, then lightly coat the surface with some of the softened butter.

Ladle onto the griddle about ¼ cup of batter, or enough to spread into a pancake about 4 inches in diameter. Quickly fill the griddle, using the same amount of batter for each pancake and leaving at least an inch or more between them.

In about a minute small bubbles will appear on the outer edges of the pancakes; in 30 seconds to a minute more, larger bubbles will appear. When the center bubbles begin to burst, quickly slide the metal spatula under each pancake, beginning with the first one poured, and gently flip them over.

Bake the second side for about half as long as the first side. You can be certain the pancakes are cooked through when almost imperceptible threads of steam begin to rise from their centers.

Do not peek at the undersides as the pancakes bake; interrupting the baking in this way may deflate them. If you feel, after baking the first batch, that the second batch would be improved by a longer or shorter time on the griddle, make the proper adjustment the second time around.

Serving the pancakes. As soon as each batch of pancakes is done, serve at once on warmed plates, 3 or 4 to a helping, overlapping them slightly in a circle. Serve them with melted butter and any of the accompaniments suggested on page 73.

BLUEBERRY PANCAKES

MAKES ABOUT 16; SERVES 4

The Blueberries
1½ cups fresh blueberries or frozen unsweetened blueberries,
    thoroughly defrosted and drained
2 tablespoons all-purpose flour

The Batter
2 cups sifted all-purpose flour
½ teaspoon salt
1 tablespoon double-acting baking powder
2 tablespoons sugar
2 eggs
1½ cups milk
4 tablespoons butter, melted but not browned

For Buttering the Griddle
2 tablespoons butter, softened at room temperature

Preparing the blueberries. If you are using fresh blueberries, wash them thoroughly under cold running water. Drain them in a colander, then spread them out on a double layer of paper towels and gently pat them dry with more towels. If you are using defrosted and drained blueberries, do not wash them; but it is essential that they be thoroughly dried, as with fresh blueberries.

Spread the dried blueberries out in a jelly-roll pan. Sprinkle them with 2 tablespoons of flour, shaking the pan from side to side to coat the berries evenly. Set the blueberries aside in the pan while you make the batter.

Preparing the batter. In a small bowl, combine 2 cups of sifted all-purpose flour, the salt, baking powder, and sugar. Stir lightly with a fork and set aside.

Break the eggs into a large mixing bowl and pour in the milk and the cooled melted butter. Using a whisk or a fork, beat them together for 8 to 10 seconds, or just until mixed.

Hold a sifter over the large mixing bowl, then pour in the flour mixture and sift it into the bowl. With a fork, stir the dry and liquid ingredients together, running the back of the fork around the sides of the bowl from time to time to dislodge any clinging flour. After a moment or so of stirring, the batter should be fairly smooth. Don't overmix it; a few small lumps in the batter will do no harm.

Preheating the griddle. Before completing the batter, preheat an electric or built-in range griddle to 400° F., or set a range-top griddle over moderate heat.

Because speed is imperative when you begin cooking the pancakes, assemble your utensils. Close by, place the softened butter, a pastry brush, a wide metal spatula, and a 2-ounce ladle or a ¼-cup dry-measuring cup.

Completing the batter. With a slotted spoon, transfer the blueberries to the batter, leaving behind any flour remaining in the pan. With a rubber spatula, gently fold the berries into the batter. Be careful not to crush the berries, or they will discolor the batter. (This will not harm the pancakes, but it will make them less attractive.)

Cooking the pancakes. Test the heat of your griddle as described on page 71, then lightly coat the surface with some of the softened butter.

Ladle onto the griddle about ¼ cup of batter, or enough to spread into a pancake about 4 inches in diameter. Ideally, the number of blueberries should be approximately the same for each pancake, but don't fuss too much about it if the berries are not evenly distributed. Quickly fill the griddle with pancakes, leaving at least an inch or more between them.

In about a minute small bubbles will appear on the outer edges of the pancakes; in 30 seconds to a minute more, larger bubbles will appear. When the center bubbles begin to burst, quickly slide the metal spatula under each pancake, beginning with the first one poured, and gently flip them over.

Bake the second side for about half as long as the first. You can be certain the pancakes are cooked through when almost imperceptible threads of steam begin to rise from their centers.

Strongly resist any temptation to peek at the undersides as the pancakes bake; interrupting the baking in this way may deflate them. If you feel, after baking the first batch, that the second batch would be improved by a longer or shorter time on the griddle, make the proper adjustment the second time around.

Before making the second batch, gently stir the batter up from the bottom with your rubber spatula to redistribute the blueberries, and brush the griddle again with more of the softened butter.

Serving the pancakes. As soon as each batch of pancakes is done, serve at once on warmed plates, 3 or 4 to a helping, overlapping them slightly in a circle instead of stacking them. Serve them with any of the accompaniments suggested on page 73.

COTTAGE-CHEESE PANCAKES

Creamed cottage cheese, the base of these delicate pancakes, varies in consistency from brand to brand. If the cheese you buy is so liquid that it won't hold its shape in a spoon, it should be drained in a sieve, then measured.

This recipe is ample for four if the pancakes are served as a dessert. For a main-course dish at luncheon or for a hearty Sunday breakfast, you may wish to double the recipe to provide second helpings.

At whatever meal you serve them, the pancakes should be accompanied by a choice of jellies or jams and each batch must be served "from pan to plate."

MAKES ABOUT 12; SERVES 4

The Batter
1 cup creamed cottage cheese that has been drained, if necessary (about ½ pound)
3 eggs
¼ cup sifted all-purpose flour
⅛ teaspoon salt
3 tablespoons butter, melted but not browned

For Buttering the Pan
3 to 4 tablespoons butter, cut into bits

Preparing the batter. Prepare the batter at least 4 hours before you plan to cook these pancakes, or even the day before. The resting period is essential to allow the batter to thicken to the proper consistency.

Place the cottage cheese in a fine-meshed sieve set over a medium-size bowl. With a rubber spatula, press the cheese against the bottom and sides of the sieve, forcing it through. Scrape any cheese clinging to the outside of the sieve into the bowl.

Break the eggs into a small bowl and beat them with a fork for a few seconds, or only long enough to combine them; do not beat them to the frothy stage. Pour the eggs slowly into the cheese, stirring constantly with the fork.

When the eggs have been completely absorbed, stir in the flour and salt. Continue to stir for 30 seconds or so, or until every trace of flour disappears. Finally, stir in the melted butter.

Cover the bowl with plastic wrap and let the batter rest at room temperature for at least 4 hours. Refrigerate the batter if you plan to let it rest overnight.

Frying the pancakes. Place about 1 tablespoon of the butter bits in a 12-inch frying pan with a nonstick surface, and set the pan over high heat. When the butter has melted but not browned and the foam begins to subside, lower the heat to moderate and quickly drop a tablespoonful of batter into the pan, repeating until the pan is filled with pancakes spaced at least 1 inch apart. The space is essential, as the batter will spread a little.

Fry the pancakes for about 2 minutes, or until pinholes appear on their surfaces and their edges show a rim of light brown. To be on the safe side, peek under one of the pancakes to check its progress. When the underside is light golden brown, quickly turn the pancakes with a small metal spatula and fry the other sides for about a minute.

Fry the succeeding batches of pancakes in the same manner, adding about a tablespoonful of butter bits to the pan for each batch.

As soon as each batch of pancakes is done, serve at once on warmed plates.

SPINACH PANCAKES

Serve Spinach Pancakes as a separate course, garnished, if you like, with slices of crisply fried bacon. Or serve them as a delicious vegetable accompaniment for any poached, broiled, or roasted meat, fish, or fowl.

For these pancakes, it makes no difference at all whether the spinach you use is frozen or freshly cooked.

MAKES 12 TO 16; SERVES 4

The Batter
One 10-ounce package frozen chopped spinach, thoroughly defrosted and drained, or ½ pound fresh spinach, cooked and thoroughly drained
2 eggs
2 egg yolks
¾ cup sifted all-purpose flour
1½ teaspoons salt
⅛ teaspoon nutmeg, preferably freshly grated
2 tablespoons butter, melted but not browned
1½ cups milk

For Buttering the Pan
4 to 6 tablespoons butter, softened at room temperature

Preparing the batter. A small handful at a time, squeeze the well-drained spinach dry. Then, using a sharp chef's knife on a chopping board, chop it very fine, almost to a purée.

Break the eggs into a 2-quart mixing bowl and add the egg yolks. Beat lightly with a fork for a few seconds, just long enough to mix the whites and yolks. Then stir in the spinach, flour, salt, nutmeg, melted butter, and milk. Continue to stir until the ingredients are thoroughly combined. Taste for seasoning. The batter may need more salt and even more nutmeg, if you like its flavor. Set the batter aside.

Preheating the oven. Line a jelly-roll pan with a double thickness of paper towels to drain the pancakes and keep them warm once they have been fried. Place the pan and serving plates in the oven, and heat the oven at the lowest possible temperature.

Because it is important that you work quickly when you start frying the pancakes, place the batter, the softened butter, a metal spatula, and a ladle or large spoon near at hand.

Frying the pancakes. Place about 2 tablespoons of the softened butter in a 12-inch frying pan with a nonstick surface, and set the pan over high heat. When the butter has melted and turned foamy but has not yet browned, lower the heat to moderate.

Fill the ladle or spoon with 2 tablespoons of spinach batter and drop it into the pan. Quickly fill the pan with pancakes, using the same amount of batter for each, and leaving at least 2 inches between pancakes. Using the metal spatula, gently flatten the pancakes into rounds about 4 inches in diameter.

Cook the pancakes for about 2 minutes, peeking under one occasionally to check its progress and regulating the heat so that the undersides become golden brown within that time. Then carefully turn the pancakes over with your spatula and fry them for about a minute more, again checking the browning once or twice. **Serving the pancakes.** Ideally, each batch of pancakes should be drained briefly on the paper-lined pan and served at once on heated plates. If you find this impractical, leave the finished pancakes in a single layer on the paper-lined jelly-roll pan in the oven while you make the rest of the pancakes.

For the second batch, add 2 more tablespoons of softened butter to the pan. It will melt and foam in seconds, so be ready to make the remaining pancakes at once. If you have batter left for a third batch, add the remaining 2 tablespoons of butter to the pan and make the rest of the pancakes.

Meanwhile, you may place the second batch of finished pancakes on the paper-lined jelly-roll pan to keep warm with the first batch, but do not leave them there more than 5 minutes. Kept any longer, the pancakes may become soggy.

GERMAN POTATO PANCAKES

These pancakes are somewhat similar to the Crispy Potato Pancakes that follow, but they are far more substantial because the batter contains both flour and baking powder, although in minimal amounts.

In the German tradition these pancakes may be served as a separate course, accompanied by individual bowls of applesauce and sour cream. As part of a main course, they go especially well with roasted or pot-roasted meats.

MAKES ABOUT 12; SERVES 4

The Potato Mixture
6 to 8 medium baking potatoes (1½ cups, packed down, after
   grating)
2 eggs
3 tablespoons finely grated onion
1½ tablespoons all-purpose flour
1 teaspoon double-acting baking powder
1 teaspoon salt
Freshly ground black pepper
2 tablespoons chopped fresh parsley

For Frying
5 to 7 tablespoons vegetable oil
5 to 7 tablespoons butter, softened at room temperature

Warming the oven. Line a jelly-roll pan with a double thickness
of paper towels to drain the pancakes and keep them warm once
they have been fried. Place the pan in the oven, together with the
serving plates, and heat the oven at the lowest possible setting.

Because it is important that you work quickly once you start
preparing the potato mixture and frying the pancakes, place the
oil and softened butter, a 1-tablespoon measuring spoon, and a
small metal spatula close at hand.

Preparing the potato mixture. Peel 6 of the potatoes and drop
each into a bowl of cold water as it is finished. When all have been
peeled, remove them one at a time, pat them dry with paper towels,
and grate them directly into a mixing bowl, using the fine-toothed
side of a stand-up four-sided grater. Work quickly to keep at a
minimum the discoloration that appears as grated potatoes stand.

When all the potatoes have been grated, squeeze them firmly,
a handful at a time, to rid them of as much moisture as possible.
As you finish squeezing each handful, drop the grated potatoes
into a pint-size glass measuring cup. You should have 1½ cups
of firmly packed grated potatoes. If not, quickly peel, grate, and
squeeze another potato or two to make the correct amount.

Without waiting a second, break the eggs into a 2-quart mixing bowl and, using a fork, beat them only long enough to mix the
whites and yolks together.

Add the grated potatoes, grated onion, flour, baking powder,
salt, a few grindings of black pepper, and the chopped parsley.
Beat the mixture with the fork until the ingredients are thor-

oughly combined. If you are not averse to the taste of raw potatoes (and there is no reason why you should be), taste the mixture for seasoning. It may well need more salt and perhaps a few more grindings of black pepper.

Frying the pancakes. Pour about 2½ tablespoons of the vegetable oil into a 12-inch frying pan with a nonstick surface. Add 2½ tablespoons of the butter, and set the pan over high heat. When the butter has begun to foam and turn faintly brown, drop a heaping tablespoonful of the potato mixture into the fat. Drop 5 more mounds of the potato mixture into the pan, spacing them well apart. With a small wide metal spatula, flatten each mound into a cake about 3 inches in diameter.

Fry the pancakes for 3 to 4 minutes, regulating the heat so that the undersides reach a deep golden brown within that time. Peek under a pancake occasionally to check its progress.

As the underside of each pancake is done, turn the pancake carefully with the spatula. Fry the second side for about the same time as the first, again periodically checking the underside for browning.

Serving the pancakes. Ideally, each batch of pancakes should be drained briefly on the paper-lined pan and served at once on warm plates. If you find this impractical, leave the pancakes in a single layer on the paper-lined pan in the warm oven while you make the rest of the pancakes.

Add 2½ tablespoons of the oil and the butter to the pan. The fats will reach the proper temperature within seconds. Proceed at once to make a second batch of pancakes.

If you have batter left, add the remaining 2 tablespoons of oil and butter to the pan and proceed to make the rest of the pancakes. Meanwhile, you may transfer the second batch to the pan in the oven, where all the pancakes may remain for no longer than 5 minutes more before serving. If left any longer, the pancakes may stay crisp, but the centers will lose the moistness they properly should have.

CRISPY POTATO PANCAKES

A bowl of applesauce and strips of bacon are good accompaniments for these crisp pancakes, which make an ideal breakfast, light luncheon, or supper dish. Served without bacon, these potato pancakes can be somewhat smaller than the 3-inch size suggested here. They make delicious morsels you can serve with drinks.

If you prefer not to serve bacon, use vegetable oil in place of the bacon fat for cooking the pancakes.

MAKES ABOUT 12; SERVES 4

The Bacon
½ pound sliced bacon

The Potato Mixture
4 to 6 medium baking potatoes (3½ cups when shredded, not packed down)
1 teaspoon salt
1 tablespoon finely cut fresh dill or 1 teaspoon dried dill weed
¼ cup finely chopped scallions, including about 2 inches of the green stems
Freshly ground black pepper

For Frying
5 tablespoons bacon fat or vegetable oil
5 tablespoons butter, softened at room temperature

Preheating the oven. Line 2 jelly-roll pans with a double thickness of paper towels to drain the bacon and pancakes and keep them warm once they have been fried. Place the pans in the oven, together with the serving plates, and heat the oven at the lowest possible setting.

Because it is important that you work fast when you prepare the potato mixture and start to fry the pancakes, place a 1-tablespoon measuring spoon, a small wide metal spatula, tongs, the softened butter, and either the vegetable oil or a small bowl and bulb baster for the bacon fat nearby at hand.

Frying the bacon. Half an hour before you intend to fry the bacon, remove it from the refrigerator and let it come to room temperature. This makes the slices easier to separate.

Arrange half the bacon slices side by side in a cold 12-inch frying pan with a nonstick surface, and set the pan over moderate heat. In a minute or two the bacon will begin to sizzle and start to release its fat. Regulate the heat so that the bacon browns slowly and evenly without burning. When the undersides are golden brown, turn the slices over with tongs. Tip the pan slightly and use the bulb baster to siphon off and transfer the accumulated fat to the nearby bowl.

Fry the second side of the bacon precisely as you did the first until it is as crisp as you like it; this is a matter of taste. Then remove the slices from the pan with tongs and place them on a paper-lined jelly-roll pan to drain and keep warm in the oven.

Fry and drain the remaining bacon in the same fashion. Pour any remaining fat into the bowl, wipe the pan with a paper towel, and set it aside while you prepare the potato mixture.

Preparing the potato mixture. Peel 4 of the potatoes and drop them into a bowl of cold water as each is finished. When the 4 potatoes have been peeled, remove them one at a time, pat them dry with paper towels, and shred them directly into a mixing bowl, using the tear-shaped teeth of a stand-up four-sided grater. Work quickly to keep at a minimum the discoloration that appears as shredded potatoes stand. (This darkening will not affect the taste of the pancakes, but it will make them decidedly less attractive.)

You should have about 3½ cups of shredded potatoes, measured without packing down in a 1-quart measuring cup. If you have less, peel and shred another potato or two to make the correct amount. Do not pour off the liquid that has accumulated in the mixing bowl or measuring cup.

Quickly return the potatoes to the mixing bowl and add the salt, dill, scallions, and a liberal grinding of black pepper. Stir together thoroughly with a fork.

Frying the pancakes. Pour 3 tablespoons of the bacon fat or vegetable oil into the 12-inch pan in which you fried the bacon. Add about 2½ tablespoons of the butter, and set the pan over high heat. When the butter has begun to foam and turn faintly brown, drop a heaping tablespoonful of the potato mixture into the fat. Fill the pan with 5 more mounds of potatoes, leaving ample space between them for turning. With the metal spatula, flatten each mound into a thin pancake about 3 inches in diameter.

Fry the pancakes for about 2 minutes, regulating the heat so that the undersides become deep golden brown within that time. Peek under a pancake occasionally to check its progress.

As each pancake is done, carefully turn it over with the spatula. Fry the second side for about the same time as the first, again checking its browning frequently. If you are not vigilant, the thin lacy edges of the pancakes may burn.

Serving the pancakes. Ideally, each batch of pancakes should be drained briefly on the paper-lined pan and served at once on warm plates, accompanied by the bacon. If this is not feasible, they may be left in the pan in the warm oven for about 5 minutes more, but no longer, while you make the rest of the pancakes. The pancakes won't lose their crisp edges if they wait longer, but their thin centers, which should be moist, will become dry if they stand too long.

Add the remaining bacon fat or oil and the butter to the pan. The fats will reach the proper temperature within seconds. Proceed at once to make pancakes with the remaining potato mixture. Drain the second batch as you did the first pancakes, and serve all of them at once.

APPLE PANCAKES

MAKES 8; SERVES 4

The Batter
4 eggs
1 cup milk
½ cup sifted all-purpose flour
2 teaspoons granulated sugar
¼ teaspoon salt

The Apple Mixture
1½ to 2 pounds tart apples, preferably Greenings (about 3¼ cups when peeled and cubed)
3 tablespoons butter, cut into bits
3 tablespoons granulated sugar
½ teaspoon powdered cinnamon

For Buttering the Pan
3 to 4 tablespoons butter, melted but not browned

The Topping
Confectioners' sugar

Preparing the batter. Break the eggs into a medium-size mixing bowl and, with a whisk, beat them for about 10 seconds. Pour in the milk and beat the eggs and milk together until they are thoroughly combined. Add the flour and continue to whisk until the batter is fairly smooth, running the whisk around the sides of the bowl from time to time to dislodge any clinging flour. A few specks or lumps of moistened flour may remain in the batter, but don't strain it. Stir in 2 teaspoons of granulated sugar and the salt. Set the bowl aside.

Preparing the apple mixture. Peel, quarter, and core 1½ pounds of apples, then cut them into ½-inch cubes. Don't fuss about making the cubes uniform—they need only be more or less the same size. You should have about 3¼ cups. If you have less, prepare more apples to make the correct amount.

Put 3 tablespoons of butter bits into a 12-inch frying pan with a nonstick surface, and set it over moderate heat. Melt the butter without letting it brown. Add the apple cubes and sprinkle them with 3 tablespoons of granulated sugar and the cinnamon. Toss and turn the apples with a rubber spatula for 2 or 3 minutes, until they have barely begun to soften. Remove the pan from the heat.

Set a sieve over a mixing bowl and, with the spatula, scrape the contents of the frying pan into the sieve and let the apples drain for a minute or two. Discard the drained liquid and turn the apples out of the sieve into the mixing bowl. Set the bowl aside.

Preheating the oven. Place a large serving platter and individual plates in the oven and turn it on at the lowest possible setting.

Because it is important to work quickly once you start frying the pancakes, place conveniently at hand the melted butter, the batter, the apples, a ½-teaspoon measuring spoon, a large spoon, a narrow metal spatula, and a 2-ounce ladle or a ¼-cup dry-measuring cup.

Frying the pancakes. Place a 6½-inch crêpe pan with a 5-inch bottom over moderate heat, and on an adjoining burner, over low heat, place a 10-inch frying pan with a nonstick surface. Test the crêpe pan for temperature, following the directions on page 37.

Pour about ½ teaspoon of melted butter into the crêpe pan, tilting the pan from side to side to spread the butter evenly. Immediately ladle about 4 tablespoons of the batter into the pan, again tilting it so that the batter covers the entire bottom of the pan.

Fry the pancake for about 1 minute, or until its surface loses most, but not all, of its glossy look. Then scatter 2 tablespoons of the apple mixture over the pancake and fry it for a few seconds longer, until its edges begin to brown.

Quickly test the larger pan for temperature, then add ½ teaspoon of melted butter to the pan. Loosen the pancake with the narrow spatula, and invert the crêpe pan over the second pan. The pancake should fall out easily, its browned side up.

Again fry the pancake for about 2 minutes, peeking under it after a few seconds. If it is browning too rapidly, lower the heat at once.

When the underside of the pancake is a light golden color, slide it onto the warmed serving platter and immediately return the platter to the oven.

Make 7 more apple pancakes in the same way, sliding each one onto the platter as it is done. Do not stack them.

Serving the pancakes. Ideally, the pancakes should be served the moment they are all finished, but you may let them remain in the warm oven for 2 or 3 minutes more if you must.

Dust the pancakes lightly with confectioners' sugar before serving them, 2 to a portion and side by side, on the warmed plates.

VARIATION: CHERRY PANCAKES

The Cherry Mixture
One 16-ounce can unsweetened pitted sour cherries
1 tablespoon butter, cut into bits
4 tablespoons sugar
½ teaspoon powdered cinnamon

Follow the preceding recipe, substituting the cherry mixture for the apple mixture. To prepare the cherry mixture, drain the cherries and discard the liquid. You should have about 1½ cups.

Put 1 tablespoon of butter bits into a 12-inch frying pan with a nonstick surface, and set it over moderate heat. Melt the butter without letting it brown. Add the cherries and sprinkle them with the sugar and the cinnamon. Toss and turn the cherries with a rubber spatula for 2 or 3 minutes, until they have barely begun to soften. Remove pan from the heat.

Set a sieve over a mixing bowl and, with the spatula, scrape the contents of the frying pan into the sieve and let the cherries drain for a minute or two. Discard the drained liquid and turn the cherries out of the sieve into the mixing bowl. Set the bowl aside while you prepare to fry the pancakes.

For each pancake, use 1 rounded tablespoon of the cherries scattered over the surface.

HUNGARIAN APRICOT PANCAKES

These delicate yet richly flavored pancakes are indubitably Hungarian in origin, although the Viennese also claim them as their own. They are called *Palatschinken* in German and *Palacsintak Barackizzel* in Hungarian. But by either name, they make a memorable finale to any meal.

MAKES 10 TO 12; SERVES 4 TO 6

The Batter
3 eggs
⅛ teaspoon salt
1 teaspoon vanilla extract
1 cup milk
1 cup sifted all-purpose flour
⅓ cup freshly opened club soda or seltzer

For Buttering the Pan
4 tablespoons butter, melted but not browned

The Filling
¾ cup apricot jam

The Topping
Confectioners' sugar
½ cup finely chopped walnuts

Preparing the batter. Break the eggs into a medium-size mixing bowl. With a whisk, beat them for about 10 seconds without allowing them to reach the frothy stage. Pour in the salt, vanilla, and milk, and beat for another 10 seconds, or until the ingredients are thoroughly combined. Then, half a cup at a time, whisk in the flour, running the whisk around the sides of the bowl every few seconds to mix in any clinging flour. Continue beating until all the flour is absorbed.

Strain the batter through a fine-meshed sieve set over a bowl, rubbing any small lumps through with the back of a spoon. Pour in the club soda or seltzer; the batter will instantly foam. Whisk it for a few seconds, just long enough to disperse the foam, before proceeding to fry the pancakes.

Frying the pancakes. Because it is important to work quickly once you start to fry the pancakes, near the stove place the batter, the melted butter, a 1-teaspoon measuring spoon, a wide metal spatula, and a 2-ounce ladle or a ¼-cup dry-measuring cup. Have a large plate close by on which to stack the pancakes as they are done.

Place an 8-inch frying pan with a nonstick surface over moderate heat. After 2 minutes, test the pan for temperature as described on page 71. Then add a teaspoon of the melted butter, tilting the pan from side to side to spread the butter evenly. Immediately pour in the slightly less than ¼ cup (2 ounces) of the batter, again tilting the pan so that the batter entirely covers the bottom.

Fry the pancake for about 2 minutes, or until the surface loses its gloss and the edges become slightly brown. Slide a metal spatula under the pancake and carefully turn it over. Fry it for about a minute more. Peek under it quickly and lower the heat if the pancake appears to be browning too deeply. Slide the finished pancake onto the waiting plate.

Immediately return the pan to the heat, add another teaspoon of butter, and pour in another measure of batter. Fry the pancake as you did the first one, stacking it, when done, on top of the first pancake. Continue frying and stacking pancakes until all the batter has been used.

Preheating the oven. Slide an oven shelf into an upper slot and preheat the oven at 400° F. for 15 minutes.

Filling the pancakes. With a pastry brush, spread a light coating of the remaining melted butter on the bottom of a shallow rectangular or oval baking-and-serving dish about 12 inches long and 8 inches wide.

In a small bowl, beat the apricot jam with a wooden spoon or a whisk until it is as smooth and fluid as possible.

Lay the pancakes out flat side by side, speckled sides up, on a long sheet of wax paper. With a rubber spatula, spread about 2 teaspoons—or more, if you like—of the beaten apricot jam over the entire top surface of each pancake.

Roll up the pancakes into fairly loose cylinders and, seam sides down, arrange them in a row, crosswise, in the buttered baking dish.

At this point you may set the dish aside, unrefrigerated and covered with plastic wrap, for up to an hour before baking.

Baking and serving the pancakes. Lightly brush the top of each rolled pancake with the remaining melted butter and place the dish in the preheated oven. Bake the pancakes for no longer than 3 minutes, or only long enough to heat them through.

Sprinkle the pancakes evenly with confectioners' sugar from a canister—or use a small sieve—and scatter the chopped walnuts over the top.

Serve the pancakes at once, 2 or 3 to a helping, on warmed plates.

Waffles: Four Versions

Waffles are, in appearance at least, among the most intriguing preparations made with batter. Handsome as they are today, they were infinitely more decorative in the twelfth century when waffles—or wafers, as they were then called—made their first appearance in Europe. In fact, waffle irons of past centuries were often as fancifully patterned as heraldic or religious emblems, and the batters baked in them were of a matching culinary complexity. Even today, some European waffle irons are made in intricate and varied patterns.

Most European waffles, unlike ours, are leavened with yeast, which gives them the texture of crisp cakes. Understandably, these cakelike waffles are often used as a base for sandwiches or sumptuous desserts. It is for this reason that Sweet-Cream Waffles are included here. Although these are not leavened with yeast, their cakelike texture will give you the opportunity to serve them as elaborately as Europeans do.

The waffles that have evolved in the United States, much like American pancakes, are simpler to prepare than the European originals. They are unsuitable for elaborate treatment and should be served simply with melted butter and maple syrup, or with brown sugar and sour cream.

The Sour-Cream Waffle recipe is essentially American in character; for variety, a version of the crisp, thin Belgian waffles made with beer is included. You will also find a regional recipe for Waffled French Toast that originated in the South. If, as a result of using these recipes, you become a waffle enthusiast, you can then continue to explore the wide world of waffles on your own.

Techniques for Making Waffles

Mixing the batter. Waffle batters made by hand are superior to those made by mechanical means. Electric mixers and blenders, however carefully controlled, tend to overdevelop the gluten in the flour, and the resulting waffles are apt to be tough rather than tender.

Keeping the batter. The waffle batters that follow, especially those containing beaten egg whites, are at their best when used immediately. The only exceptions might be batters made with whole eggs that may rest, if they must, for 15 minutes or so before baking.

Heating the waffle maker. If your waffle iron is a new one, read the manufacturer's instructions for using and caring for it. Some irons—even those that are coated with a nonstick surface—may require seasoning with oil or other fat before the first use.

Although all electric waffle irons are equipped with thermostats that indicate when they have reached the proper temperature for cooking, you would be wise to test the temperature before pouring in the batter. And, of course, if you are using a range-top waffle iron, whether an heirloom or a European import, you *must* check its temperature.

To test the heat, simply flick a few drops of cold water on the opened heated grids; they should steam for a second or two before vanishing. If the drops sizzle and evaporate instantly, the iron is too hot; if they steam sluggishly, it is not hot enough. Raise or lower the heat as needed until another few drops of water flicked onto the surface behave as they should.

Buttering the waffle iron. If your waffle iron has a nonstick surface, it is undesirable to butter the grids because the butter tends to pool instead of spreading over them. If yours is a plain waffle iron—that is, one that does not have a nonstick surface—coat it with softened or melted butter, using a pastry brush.

Measuring the batter. Because waffle batters vary in denseness, the amount of batter for each type of waffle depends on its particular recipe. Some waffle batters are quite thick and fluffy; some are fairly thick but not too dense to prevent you from seeing the grid pattern as the batter spreads in the iron; and some are quite thin. Each recipe indicates how full of batter the iron should be before baking.

A little practice with your waffle maker and a specific batter will soon show you the exact quantity to use to make waffles the way you like them. In general, the more batter you pour into the iron, the thicker your finished waffle will be.

Cooking the waffles. Most manufacturers' manuals accompanying electric waffle irons indicate that a waffle is done when steam no longer emerges from between the grids at the sides of the iron. This is only a general indication, to be coupled with the timing directions in the following recipes and your own experience with your particular appliance.

Bear in mind that you should never open the waffle iron to peek until the waffle has baked at least 3 minutes; to open it sooner will certainly damage the waffle and cause it to stick. Follow the timing directions in each recipe precisely, then adjust the baking time of the second and subsequent waffles, if you like, to get the shade of brown and the degree of crispness you prefer.

Serving the waffles. To be at their best, these waffles should ideally be served on warmed plates the moment they are done. An exception might be small triangles of Waffled French Toast, baked crisp to be served with drinks, which will keep their crispness for 10 to 15 minutes.

Because waffles tend to cool rapidly when served on cold plates, warm the serving plates in an oven that has been preheated at the lowest possible temperature, or in a dishwasher with a plate-warming setting.

SOUR-CREAM WAFFLES

Any of the accompaniments suggested on page 73 for American Pancakes—melted butter, maple syrup, honey, and honey-butter cream—would go equally well with these paradoxically substantial yet delicately textured waffles. Crisp bacon would be suitable too, if you intend to serve the waffles for a winter breakfast or lunch.

SERVES 4

The Batter
1½ cups sifted cake flour
1½ teaspoons double-acting baking powder
¾ teaspoon baking soda
½ teaspoon salt
2 teaspoons sugar
4 egg yolks
1 pint sour cream
½ cup milk
4 tablespoons butter, melted but not browned
4 egg whites

For Buttering the Waffle Iron (without a nonstick surface)
2 tablespoons butter, softened at room temperature

Preheating the waffle iron. Set the control of your electric waffle iron for medium heat.

Preparing the batter. In a small bowl combine the cake flour, baking powder, baking soda, salt, and sugar. Stir together with a fork and set aside.

Place the egg yolks, sour cream, milk, and 4 tablespoons of melted butter in a medium-size mixing bowl and, with a whisk, beat them together for about 10 seconds, or just long enough to blend them.

Hold a sifter over the mixing bowl, then pour in the flour mixture and sift it into the bowl. Beat the dry and liquid ingredients together with the whisk, running the whisk around the sides of the bowl from time to time to dislodge any clinging flour. Continue to beat for 30 seconds or so, or until the batter is smooth.

With a rotary beater, beat the egg whites in a medium-size glass or stainless-steel bowl until they form firm peaks on the beater when it is lifted upright above the bowl.

With a rubber spatula, immediately scrape the beaten whites over the batter and fold them in, cutting down through the whites and the batter, then lifting the heavier mass of batter repeatedly over the whites. Run the spatula across the bottom and around the sides of the bowl occasionally, just until no streaks of whites show. Be careful not to overfold, or you will lose the air you have beaten into the egg whites. The batter will be fluffy and rather thick.

Pour the batter immediately into a quart-size glass measuring cup or a pitcher.

Baking the waffles. Test the waffle iron for temperature as described on page 93. If you are using an iron without a nonstick surface, brush the grids evenly with some of the softened butter, using a pastry brush, before baking each waffle.

Pour enough batter over the grids to cover most but not quite all of the area; the batter-covered section will expand to fill the remaining space as soon as the iron is closed. Without waiting a second, close the waffle iron.

In a moment or so you will see small jets of steam puffing their way between the grids of the iron. But don't be tempted to open the iron until the batter has baked for at least 3 minutes; if you do, the batter will surely stick to the grids.

When the steaming has stopped, the waffle is done for most tastes. You may now check the browning; if the waffle is lighter in color than you like, close the iron and let the waffle bake for another moment.

Serving the waffles. With a fork, carefully remove the waffle and place it on a warmed plate. Divide the waffle into sections, if you wish, and serve it at once with whatever accompaniments you prefer.

Bake and serve the remaining waffles in precisely the same fashion.

BEER-BATTER WAFFLES

You will notice when you make these waffles that their upper sides will usually brown unevenly. This is a singular characteristic of this batter made with beer, but you can cope with it easily enough: Simply serve the waffles with their more attractive side up.

I think these crisp waffles are at their best when presented with a bowl of soft dark-brown sugar and another bowl of chilled sour cream. However, you may, if you wish, serve them with one of the more conventional accompaniments for American Pancakes suggested on page 73.

The Batter
1½ cups sifted all-purpose flour
1 tablespoon sugar
¼ teaspoon salt
4 eggs
1½ cups beer (a 12-ounce can), poured into a bowl and allowed to rest for 5 minutes for the foam to subside
2 tablespoons vegetable oil
2 tablespoons butter, melted but not browned
1 teaspoon strained fresh lemon juice

For Buttering the Waffle Iron (without a nonstick surface)
2 tablespoons butter, softened at room temperature

Preheating the waffle iron. Set the control of your waffle iron for medium heat.
Preparing the batter. In a small bowl combine the flour, sugar, and salt. Stir together lightly with a fork and set the bowl aside.

Break the eggs into a large mixing bowl and pour in the beer, oil, 2 tablespoons of melted butter, and the lemon juice. With a whisk, beat together for about 2 minutes.

Hold a sifter over the mixing bowl, then add the flour mixture and sift it into the bowl. Stir the dry and liquid ingredients together with the whisk, running it around the sides of the bowl from time to time to dislodge any clinging flour. After a moment or so of stirring, the batter will be smooth and quite thin—about the consistency of medium cream.

Pour the batter into a quart-size glass measuring cup or a pitcher. It can rest for up to 15 minutes if necessary, but baking it at once will produce crisper, lighter waffles.
Baking the waffles. Test the waffle iron for temperature as described on page 93. If you are using an iron without a nonstick surface, brush the grids evenly with softened butter, using a pastry brush, before baking each waffle.

Pour enough batter over the grids to cover them completely—in fact, until the iron will hold no more batter without overflowing. Immediately close the cover.

In a moment or so you will see small jets of steam puffing out between the grids. But don't open the iron until the batter has baked for at least 3 minutes; if you open it sooner, the batter will surely stick to the grids. A typical baking time for these waffles is 5 minutes in all. If you wish, you can, of course, lengthen or shorten the time to brown the waffles to your taste.

Serving the waffles. With a fork, carefully remove the waffle and place it on a warmed plate. Serve the waffle at once, divided into sections, if you wish, together with any of the accompaniments I suggest at the head of the recipe.

Bake and serve the remaining waffles in the same way.

SWEET-CREAM WAFFLES

Although you may serve these cakelike waffles with conventional accompaniments—melted butter, maple syrup, honey, honey-butter cream, bacon, brown sugar, sour cream—they readily lend themselves to more elaborate treatment. They can be topped with any of the fillings described in the crêpe section of this book, the amount of filling depending on how lavish you want the dish to be. And you can easily use the waffles as the base for opulent desserts of your own devising, mounding each waffle with sweetened whipped cream and topping the cream with strawberries, raspberries, or any other fresh, cooked, or preserved fruit you wish.

SERVES 4

The Batter
1½ cups sifted cake flour
1 tablespoon double-acting baking powder
½ teaspoon salt
1 teaspoon sugar
3 egg yolks
1 cup heavy cream
4 tablespoons butter, melted but not browned
3 egg whites

For Buttering the Waffle Iron (without a nonstick surface)
2 tablespoons butter, softened at room temperature

Preheating the waffle iron. Set the control of your electric waffle iron for medium heat.

Preparing the batter. In a small bowl combine the sifted cake flour, baking powder, salt, and sugar. Stir lightly with a fork and set aside.

Place the egg yolks, cream, and 4 tablespoons of melted butter in a medium-size mixing bowl and, with a whisk, beat them together for about 10 seconds.

Hold a sifter over the mixing bowl, then pour in the flour mixture and sift it into the bowl. Beat the dry and liquid ingredients together, running the whisk around the sides of the bowl from time to time to dislodge any clinging flour. Then continue to beat for 30 seconds or so, or until the batter is quite smooth.

With a rotary beater, beat the egg whites in a medium-size glass or stainless-steel bowl until they form firm peaks on the beater when it is lifted upright.

With a rubber spatula, immediately scrape the beaten whites over the batter and fold them in, cutting down through the batter and the egg whites and lifting the heavier mass of batter repeatedly over the whites. As you fold, run the spatula across the bottom and around the sides of the bowl occasionally until no streaks of whites show. Be careful not to overfold, or you will lose the air you have beaten into the egg whites. The batter will be fluffy and very thick.

Pour the batter immediately into a quart-size glass measuring cup or a pitcher.

Baking the waffles. Test the waffle iron for temperature as described on page 93. If you are using an iron without a nonstick surface, brush the grids evenly with some of the softened butter, using a pastry brush, before baking each waffle.

Pour about ⅔ cup of the batter into the center of the grid, and, because the thick batter does not flow readily, with a rubber spatula spread the batter to within an inch of the outside edges of the grid. Immediately close the waffle iron. Let the waffle bake for about 4 minutes before opening the iron; do not be tempted to peek any sooner. If the waffle is not brown enough for your taste, close the iron and bake it for another minute or so.

Serving the waffles. With a fork, carefully remove the waffle and place it on a warmed plate. Divide the waffle into sections, if you wish, and serve it at once with whatever accompaniments you may prefer.

Bake and serve the remaining waffles in the same way.

WAFFLED FRENCH TOAST

Ordinarily, commercially baked soft white bread is useless, but here is one recipe for which it is essential. Because it has the singular property of soaking up batter like a sponge—and for this reason alone—it is more effective for Waffled French Toast than home-baked bread or any of the superior brands of packaged white bread.

Waffled French Toast makes an excellent accompaniment for drinks of any kind. If you plan to use it for that purpose, cut the bread triangles in half again, and bake these smaller triangles to a decidedly crisp stage.

SERVES 4

The Bread
8 slices of white bread of the soft, spongy type

The Batter
4 eggs
6 tablespoons heavy cream
½ teaspoon salt
4 tablespoons butter, melted but not browned

For Buttering the Waffle Iron (without a nonstick surface)
2 tablespoons butter, softened at room temperature

Preheating the waffle iron. Set the control of your electric waffle iron for medium heat.
Preparing the bread. With a large sharp knife, trim the crusts from 8 slices of bread, then cut each slice in half on the diagonal.
Making the batter. Break the eggs into a medium-size bowl, and add the cream, salt, and 4 tablespoons of melted butter. Beat the ingredients with a whisk for about 20 seconds, or only until combined.

Pour the batter into a shallow dish large enough to hold 4 triangles of bread in one layer.
Baking the waffled French toast. For the first batch of waffles, place 4 of the bread triangles in the batter. Let them soak for a moment, just until they have absorbed as much of the batter as they can hold without softening too much.

Test the waffle iron for temperature as described on page 93. If you are using an iron without a nonstick surface, brush the grids evenly with some of the softened butter, using a pastry brush.

With a slotted spatula, carefully lift up the batter-soaked bread triangles one at a time and place them on the waffle iron. If the triangles seem misshapen or start to fall apart before baking, pat them into shape with your spatula.

Bake the toast for 2 minutes, then cautiously open the iron to see if the slices are the color you like. If they are too pale, close the iron and bake a minute or so longer.

Serving the waffled French toast. With a fork, remove the triangles from the iron and serve them at once on a warmed plate.

Soak and bake the remaining bread triangles in the same way and serve them the moment each batch is done.

VARIATION: WAFFLED FRENCH CHEESE TOAST

For an interesting variation in flavor in the Waffled French Toast, add 4 tablespoons of freshly grated imported Parmesan cheese to the batter, then bake as described in the preceding recipe. Serve these cheese-flavored waffles for luncheon or a light supper with melted butter and a sprinkling of additional Parmesan cheese. A particularly fine accompaniment for drinks are the smaller triangles baked to a crisp and sprinkled with a little more Parmesan cheese.

SOUFFLÉS:
ELEGANT AND
UNTEMPERAMENTAL

*T*he magic of the egg was never more perfectly demonstrated than in that bit of culinary legerdemain conceived by the French—the soufflé. Soufflé comes from *souffler*, meaning "to breathe," "to inflate," "to puff up," and one cannot help but wonder what inspired chef first whipped egg whites to a stiff shiny "snow," folded them into a thick sauce, then baked the mixture.

A soufflé can be many things. It can be savory or sweet, an hors d'oeuvre, an entrée, or a dessert. But it is always cooked, almost always served hot, and it usually depends on properly beaten egg whites to push it to dazzling heights. One notable exception is the Soufflé Chocolate Roll, a kind of "failed" soufflé that is baked in a large shallow pan rather than a soufflé dish or mold, and is intentionally left to fall and cool so it can be rolled up and served like a jelly roll.

Most cold soufflés, sometimes called iced or frozen soufflés, are actually mousses and not true soufflés. These are discussed in the next section, "Mousses and Creams."

The true soufflé, one of the glories of French cuisine, is actually easy to make, although there are even experienced cooks who are convinced it can be achieved only by a culinary magician or, at the very least, by a great French chef. The secret lies in the egg whites. And once you have learned to make the Basic Cheese

Soufflé—the easiest of all to make—you have, in a sense, learned to make all soufflés, whether savory or sweet.

Techniques for Making Soufflés

Choosing the soufflé dish. Although you can bake a soufflé in any ovenproof dish about 3 inches deep, the most attractive ones are the straight-sided porcelain soufflé dish, the glass soufflé mold, and the cylindrical metal mold called a charlotte. The three most useful sizes are 1 quart, 1½ quarts, and 2 quarts.

A savory soufflé in a 1-quart mold would probably serve only 2 people as a main course, and a 1½-quart soufflé might serve 4. But a vegetable soufflé in a 1½-quart mold accompanying an entrée would probably serve 6. Dessert soufflés usually go further. If you want more servings than a recipe will yield, don't double the recipe; make two soufflés. And never make a recipe that calls for a soufflé dish larger than 2 quarts (8 cups)—it will not cook within the given length of time.

Preparing the soufflé dish. With a pastry brush or a piece of wax paper, butter the bottom and sides of the dish fairly heavily, making certain the butter gets into the crease at the bottom. Then spoon a couple of tablespoons of the coating ingredient into the buttered mold. This may be grated cheese, fine dry bread crumbs, flour, or sugar (and sometimes a combination of the last two), depending on the type of soufflé; the recipe will specify the coating.

Roll the dish around and around in your hands to coat the insides and bottom evenly but lightly. Turn the mold upside down to discard any surplus coating.

Professional chefs chill a prepared soufflé dish at least 30 minutes to help the hot soufflé not only to rise, but to rise straight up. If you are in a hurry, chill the dish in the freezer.

Incorporating the egg whites. Generally speaking, French soufflé recipes call for at least one extra egg white to 4 whole eggs, in contrast to American recipes, which often use the same number of whites as yolks. In professional kitchens, chefs add extra egg whites almost at will. Obviously, the capacity of your soufflé dish will eventually limit you, but three extra egg whites are not unusual.

The secret of a soufflé lies in the egg whites, or rather, the air beaten into them that expands as the soufflé bakes, giving it its impressive height. Traditionalists recommend the big balloon whip (*fouet*, in French) and an unlined copper bowl, believing that egg whites mount faster and with greater volume, but modern beaters—the rotary, the electric, and particularly the big electric mixer—are marvelously effective pieces of equipment that, to a large extent, take the work out of cooking. If you don't have a copper bowl, use a glass or stainless-steel bowl; aluminum will turn your whites gray, and most plastic bowls will decrease their volume.

Properly beaten egg whites can mount to seven or eight times their original volume; they are smooth and glistening (sometimes called "wet"), free from granules, and they will hold firm, glossy peaks when the beater is lifted straight up. If egg whites are granular or dry, they have been overbeaten and will have lost much of their air; the soufflé will not rise properly. You might note here that whatever else you may have heard, there is little difference in volume and stiffness between egg whites at room temperature and those that are cold when you beat them.

To fold the fragile beaten egg whites into the heavier soufflé base without losing too much air, add about a cup of the beaten egg whites to the soufflé base and whip them in vigorously with a wire whip. This lightens the mixture and makes folding easier. Then, using a rubber spatula, scoop the soufflé base on top of the remaining egg whites and cut down from the top center of the mixture to the bottom of the bowl. Next, draw the spatula toward you against the edge of the bowl, rotating the bowl as you work. Working quickly, repeat the cutting, folding, and rotating until the whites have been incorporated, but do not be too thorough; it is better to have a few unblended patches of egg white than a soufflé that won't rise.

Filling the soufflé dish. Because soufflés rise so dramatically during baking, allow plenty of room in the dish or mold for expansion. Dessert soufflés, in particular, being more delicate than the savory kind, very nearly double in volume. A good rule of thumb in filling a soufflé dish is to allow at least 1½ inches at the top, and 2 inches if the soufflé mixture seems unusually soft and light.

Baking the soufflé. For the most even distribution of heat, cook the soufflé on a baking sheet on an oven shelf at a middle level of a preheated oven. Heat the baking sheet in the oven during the preheating so that the soufflé resting on it will start to cook at the bottom as well as at the top. This way you won't have an overly liquid layer in the bottom of the soufflé.

Most soufflés are baked in 25 to 30 minutes, or when the soufflé has risen 2 to 3 inches above its original level. However, there are some soufflés—particularly vegetable, fish, meat, and chocolate—

that never rise that high because the egg whites don't have the power to lift those heavy mixtures beyond a certain point.

If you like a creamy center, bake your soufflé a few minutes less than the time indicated in the recipe. The soufflé is still creamy if the top quivers when you gently move the soufflé dish.

Serving the soufflé. As everybody knows, a soufflé waits for no one and must be served the minute it comes from the oven. Place the hot soufflé on top of a folded napkin on your serving tray or platter. The napkin not only makes an attractive presentation, but also helps to keep the soufflé from sliding around during the serving.

To serve it properly, puncture the top of the soufflé with a serving spoon and fork held straight up and back to back, then gently spread the soufflé apart for each portion.

BASIC CHEESE SOUFFLÉ

SERVES 3 TO 4

For Preparing the Soufflé Dish
1 tablespoon butter, softened at room temperature
2 tablespoons freshly grated Parmesan cheese

The Soufflé Mixture
3 tablespoons butter, cut into bits
3 tablespoons flour
1 cup milk
4 egg yolks
¾ cup freshly grated Switzerland cheese or half Switzerland
   and half Parmesan cheese (about ¼ pound total); or ⅔
   cup grated natural Cheddar cheese
⅝ teaspoon salt
Pinch of freshly ground white pepper
Pinch of cayenne pepper
Pinch of freshly grated nutmeg
7 egg whites
⅛ teaspoon cream of tartar

Preparing the soufflé dish. Butter a 1½-quart soufflé dish or charlotte mold with 1 tablespoon of softened butter. Then coat the inside surfaces evenly with 2 tablespoons of grated Parmesan cheese and discard the surplus. Refrigerate the dish for at least 30 minutes.

Preheating the oven. Slide an oven shelf into a center slot, place a baking sheet in the center of it, and preheat the oven at 400° F. for 15 minutes.

Making the soufflé base. Place 3 tablespoons of butter bits in a heavy 2-quart saucepan and set the pan over low heat. When the butter has melted but not browned, remove the pan from the heat. Add the flour and stir vigorously with a wooden spoon until the mixture—the roux—is smooth. Then pour in the milk. With a whisk, beat the milk and roux together until they are fairly well combined.

Set the pan over high heat and, whisking constantly, bring the sauce to a boil. When it is thick and smooth, lower the heat and, stirring frequently, cook slowly for 1 or 2 minutes. Remove the pan from the heat.

One at a time, quickly whisk in the egg yolks. Add the ¾ cup of grated cheese, ½ teaspoon of the salt, the white pepper, cayenne pepper, and the nutmeg, and mix thoroughly with a wooden spoon or whisk until the sauce is smooth. Taste the sauce for seasoning; it may need more salt. Remember that a soufflé base should be slightly overseasoned if the soufflé is to have any character when the beaten egg whites are added. Set the soufflé base aside while you beat the egg whites.

At this point you may set the soufflé base aside for up to 12 hours, tightly covered with plastic wrap and refrigerated. In that case, heat it gently to lukewarm before proceeding with the recipe.

Making the soufflé. Put the egg whites in the bowl of your electric mixer or, if you are using a rotary beater or a large whisk, in a large glass, stainless-steel, or copper bowl. Add the remaining ⅛ teaspoon of salt and the cream of tartar. Beat the egg whites until they hold firm, glossy peaks when the beater is lifted straight up.

With a wire whisk, beat about a cup of the whites vigorously into the warm soufflé base. Then, using a rubber spatula, reverse the process and scrape the soufflé base over the remaining whites. Gently combine them, using the spatula to cut and fold the mixture as you rotate the bowl. Fold gently just until no streaks of egg white show, but be particularly careful not to overfold or the soufflé won't rise as it should.

Baking and serving the soufflé. Pour the soufflé mixture into the prepared dish, smooth the surface with the spatula, and place the dish in the center of the baking sheet in the oven. Immediately turn the heat down to 375° F. and bake for 25 to 30 minutes, or until the soufflé has puffed above the dish and browned lightly. For a firm rather than a creamy center, bake the soufflé an additional 5 minutes. Serve at once.

OYSTER SOUFFLÉ

SERVES 4

For Preparing the Soufflé Dish
1 tablespoon butter, softened at room temperature
2 tablespoons freshly grated Parmesan cheese

For Preparing the Oysters
18 fresh oysters in their liquor
Milk, up to 1 cup
½ cup freshly grated Parmesan cheese
⅓ cup olive oil
1 small clove garlic, peeled and minced
12 oyster crackers, pulverized in an electric blender or food
     processor
⅛ teaspoon freshly ground white pepper

The Soufflé Mixture
4 tablespoons butter, cut into bits
4 tablespoons flour
6 egg yolks
⅜ teaspoon salt
⅛ teaspoon freshly ground white pepper
9 egg whites
⅛ teaspoon cream of tartar

The Topping
2 tablespoons freshly grated Parmesan cheese

Preparing the soufflé dish. Butter a 2-quart soufflé dish with 1 tablespoon of softened butter. Then coat the inside surfaces evenly with 2 tablespoons of grated Parmesan cheese. Refrigerate the dish for at least 30 minutes.

Preparing the oysters. Place the oysters in a large sieve set over a bowl and allow them to drain thoroughly. Stir them occasionally to encourage draining.

Place 6 of the drained oysters in the container of an electric blender or food processor. Add the drained oyster liquor and purée at high speed. Pour the contents of the container into a 1-cup measure. If the oyster liquid does not fill the cup, add enough milk to give you full measure. Set the oyster liquid aside to use in making the soufflé base.

Coating the oysters. Line a baking sheet with wax paper or paper toweling. Nearby, place ½ cup of grated Parmesan cheese in one small bowl, the olive oil mixed with the minced garlic in another, and the cracker crumbs well mixed with ⅛ teaspoon of white pepper in the third. Take 1 oyster at a time, dry it with paper toweling, then dip it first into the grated cheese, next into the oil-garlic combination, and finally roll it in cracker crumbs. Shake each oyster gently over the bowl of crumbs to rid it of any loose crumbs, then place it on the paper-lined pan. When all 12 oysters are crumbed, refrigerate them until needed so that the crumb coating will stick.

Preheating the oven. Slide an oven shelf into a center slot, place a baking sheet in the center of it, and preheat the oven at 375° F. for 15 minutes.

Making the soufflé base. Place 4 tablespoons of butter bits in a heavy 2-quart saucepan and set the pan over low heat. When the butter has melted but not browned, remove the pan from the heat. Add the flour and stir vigorously with a wooden spoon until the mixture—the roux—is smooth. Then pour in the oyster liquid. With a whisk, beat until they are fairly well combined.

Set the pan over high heat and, whisking constantly, bring the sauce to a boil. When it is thick, lower the heat and, stirring frequently, cook slowly for 1 or 2 minutes. Remove the pan from the heat.

One at a time, whisk in the egg yolks. Then add ¼ teaspoon of the salt and ⅛ teaspoon of white pepper, and mix well. Set the soufflé base aside while you beat the egg whites.

Making the soufflé. Put the egg whites in the bowl of your electric mixer or, if you are using a rotary beater or a large whisk, in a large glass, stainless-steel, or copper bowl. Add the remaining ⅛ teaspoon of salt and the cream of tartar. Beat the egg whites until they hold firm, glossy peaks when the beater is lifted straight up.

With a wire whisk, beat about a cup of the whites vigorously into the warm soufflé base. Then, using a rubber spatula, reverse the process and scrape the soufflé base over the remaining whites. Gently combine them, using the spatula to cut and fold the mixture as you rotate the bowl. Fold gently just until no streaks of egg white show.

Baking and serving the soufflé. Pour half the soufflé mixture into the prepared soufflé dish. Arrange the 12 crumbed oysters on top, all in one layer, and cover with the remaining soufflé mixture. Smooth the surface with a rubber spatula and sprinkle the top with 2 tablespoons of grated Parmesan cheese (and any cheese remaining in the bowl from coating the oysters).

Place the soufflé in the center of the hot baking sheet in the preheated oven, and bake for 30 to 35 minutes, or until the top is puffed and golden.

Serve the soufflé the instant it comes from the oven, making sure that every person gets some of the crumbed oysters.

INDIVIDUAL CRABMEAT SOUFFLÉS

Lump crabmeat is the most expensive and also the most desirable when appearance is important. In a dish such as this, however, it is practical to use the less expensive regular or "flake" crabmeat.

SERVES 8

For Preparing the Scallop Shells
2 tablespoons butter, softened at room temperature
2 tablespoons finely grated Parmesan cheese

The Soufflé Mixture
3 tablespoons butter, cut into bits
3 tablespoons flour
1 cup milk
1 egg yolk
4 tablespoons freshly grated Parmesan cheese
¼ teaspoon dry mustard
2 to 3 teaspoons strained fresh lemon juice
8 to 10 drops Tabasco
½ pound fresh "flake" crabmeat
6 egg whites
½ teaspoon salt
⅛ teaspoon cream of tartar

The Topping
2 tablespoons freshly grated Parmesan cheese

Preparing the scallop shells. With 2 tablespoons of softened butter, generously grease the insides of 8 scallop shells, each measuring 4½ to 5 inches across. Place the shells on a large piece of wax paper. Pour 2 tablespoons of grated Parmesan cheese into a small sieve and sift it over the shells to coat the insides well. Turn each shell over to rid it of any excess cheese, then place it on a jelly-roll pan or baking sheet and refrigerate for 30 minutes.
Preheating the oven. Slide an oven shelf in a center slot, place a baking sheet on it, and preheat the oven at 425° F. for 15 minutes.
Making the soufflé base. Place 3 tablespoons of butter bits in a heavy 2-quart saucepan and set the pan over low heat. When the butter has melted but not browned, remove the pan from the heat. Add the flour and stir vigorously with a wooden spoon until the mixture—the roux—is smooth. Then pour in the milk. With a whisk, beat the milk and roux together until they are fairly well combined.

Set the pan over high heat and, whisking constantly, bring the sauce to a boil. When it is thick and smooth, lower the heat and, stirring frequently, cook slowly for 1 or 2 minutes. Remove pan from the heat.

Whisk in the egg yolk. Add 4 tablespoons of grated Parmesan cheese, the dry mustard, 2 teaspoons of the lemon juice, and 8 drops of the Tabasco, and stir until the sauce is smooth. At this point taste the sauce for seasoning; it may need the remaining teaspoon of lemon juice and the 2 extra drops of Tabasco. Remember that this soufflé base should be slightly overseasoned if the soufflé is to have any character when the beaten egg whites are added.

Pick over the crabmeat carefully to remove any cartilage and bits of shell, then shred the meat very fine with a fork. If the crab seems too damp (this is unlikely), pat it dry with paper towels. Mix the crabmeat into the soufflé base.

Making the soufflé. Put the egg whites in the bowl of your electric mixer or, if you are using a rotary beater or a large whisk, in a large glass, stainless-steel, or copper bowl. Add the salt and cream of tartar. Beat the egg whites until they hold firm, glossy peaks when the beater is lifted straight up.

With a wire whisk, beat about a cup of the whites vigorously into the soufflé base. Then, using a rubber spatula, reverse the process and scrape the soufflé base over the remaining whites. Gently combine them, using the spatula to cut and fold the mixture as you rotate the bowl. Fold gently just until no streaks of egg white show.

Filling the scallop shells. Spoon 2 heaping tablespoons of the soufflé mixture into the center of each prepared scallop shell. Then divide the remainder evenly among the 8 shells, piling it high in the center. Do not attempt to smooth the surface. When all the shells are filled, sprinkle 2 tablespoons of grated Parmesan cheese over the tops of the soufflés.

Baking and serving the soufflés. Pull out the center oven shelf and, working fast so you won't lose oven heat, transfer the individual scallop shells to the hot baking sheet in the oven. Reduce the heat to 400° F. and bake the soufflés for 12 to 15 minutes, or until they have puffed and are lightly golden.

As soon as the soufflés are done, place on individual serving plates and serve as a first course.

LOBSTER SOUFFLÉ WITH LOBSTER SAUCE

SERVES 4

For Preparing the Soufflé Dish
1 tablespoon butter, softened at room temperature
2 tablespoons flour

The Lobster Mixture
1 live lobster, 2 to 2½ pounds
2 tablespoons olive oil
2 tablespoons butter, softened at room temperature
½ teaspoon salt
⅛ teaspoon freshly ground white pepper
3 shallots or scallion bulbs, peeled and coarsely chopped
2 tablespoons coarsely chopped yellow onion (about ½ small
     yellow onion)
1 clove garlic, peeled and crushed
¼ cup Cognac
2 cups (1 pint) clam juice
½ cup dry white wine
2 tablespoons tomato paste
2 fresh tomatoes, coarsely chopped (no need to peel or core)
1 tablespoon chopped fresh tarragon or 1 teaspoon crumbled
     dried tarragon
3 sprigs parsley
⅛ teaspoon cayenne pepper

The Lobster Sauce
2 tablespoons butter, softened at room temperature
2 tablespoons flour
½ cup dry white wine
¼ cup heavy cream
2 tablespoons Cognac

The Soufflé Mixture
2 tablespoons butter, cut into bits
2 tablespoons flour
1 cup milk
4 egg yolks
2 tablespoons grated Gruyère cheese (1 ounce)
⅜ teaspoon salt
⅛ teaspoon freshly ground white pepper
6 egg whites
⅛ teaspoon cream of tartar

Preparing the soufflé dish. Butter a 2-quart soufflé dish with 1 tablespoon of softened butter. Then coat the inside surfaces evenly with 2 tablespoons of flour. Refrigerate the dish for at least 30 minutes.

Cutting up the lobster. The man at your fish market can cut up and clean the lobster for you, but it isn't difficult to do.

First, kill the lobster by inserting a heavy, sharp knife through the back between the body and tail shells. This cuts the spinal column and dispatches the lobster quickly.

In order to salvage any liquid from the lobster, cut it up over a large pan or bowl. With the same heavy knife, cut off the tail section, crosswise, where it joins the body, and remove the intestinal vein, which runs the length of the tail. Cut the tail section at the joints into 4 or 5 pieces. Cut off the claws, cracking them with the back of the knife or with a hammer.

Split the body in half lengthwise, removing and discarding the stomach (the small sac between the eyes) and the upper part of the intestinal vein. Reserve the lobster juice. Set aside the tomalley (liver), which is green, and the coral, if any, which is also green but which turns red when cooked.

Cooking the lobster mixture. Combine the olive oil and 2 tablespoons of butter in a heavy 12-inch frying pan, preferably one with a nonstick surface, that has a tight-fitting lid. Place the pan over high heat until the butter has melted and is very hot, but has not browned. Add the lobster and sauté, turning the pieces with tongs, for 3 to 4 minutes, or until the shells turn bright red. Sprinkle with ½ teaspoon of salt and ⅛ teaspoon of white pepper. Reduce the heat to moderate. Add the shallots or scallions, the yellow onion, and the garlic, and mix well with a wooden spoon. Add ¼ cup of Cognac and ignite with a match. Shake the pan until the flames die out completely.

Add the clam juice, ½ cup of white wine, tomato paste, fresh tomatoes, tarragon, parsley, and the cayenne pepper, and stir well.

Bring the mixture to a boil, then reduce the heat to low, cover the pan, and simmer for 15 minutes. With tongs, lift the pieces of lobster to a pan or platter to cool, and set the frying pan with the rest of the lobster mixture aside, to use in making the lobster sauce.

Shelling the lobster. When cool enough to handle, take the lobster meat out of the shells, using a pick or small knife to extricate the bits and pieces. Cut the meat into bite-size pieces and set them aside; discard the shells.

Making the lobster sauce. In a small bowl and using a fork, mix the reserved lobster liquid, tomalley, and coral with 2 tablespoons of softened butter, 2 tablespoons of flour, and ½ cup of white wine. Scrape this into the frying pan and combine it with the lobster mixture, using a whisk or a wooden spoon. Place the frying pan over low heat and, stirring occasionally, cook, uncovered, for 20 minutes, or until the sauce has reduced to about 1½ cups.

Set a fine sieve over a small mixing bowl and strain the sauce, pressing with a rubber spatula to extract all the liquid. Measure out 1 cup of the sauce and combine it with the reserved lobster meat, then set it aside to use in making the soufflé. Pour the remaining sauce into a small heavy saucepan and set it aside to use in finishing the lobster sauce, about 5 minutes before the soufflé is done.

Preheating the oven. Slide an oven shelf into a center slot, place a baking sheet in the middle of it, and preheat the oven at 375° F. for 15 minutes.

Making the soufflé base. Place 2 tablespoons of butter bits in a heavy 2-quart saucepan and set the pan over low heat. When the butter has melted but not browned, remove the pan from the heat. Add 2 tablespoons of flour and stir vigorously with a wooden spoon until the mixture—the roux—is smooth. Pour in the milk. With a whisk, beat the milk and roux together until they are fairly well combined.

Set the pan over high heat and, whisking constantly, bring the sauce to a boil. When it is thick and smooth, lower the heat and, stirring frequently, cook slowly for 1 or 2 minutes. Remove the pan from the heat.

One at a time whisk in the egg yolks. Stir in the cheese, ¼ teaspoon of the salt, and ⅛ teaspoon of white pepper, and whisk until the sauce is smooth. Set the soufflé base aside.

Making the soufflé. Put the egg whites in the bowl of your electric mixer or, if you are using a rotary beater or a large wire whisk, in a large glass, stainless-steel, or copper bowl. Add the remaining ⅛ teaspoon of salt, and the cream of tartar. Beat the egg whites until they hold firm, glossy peaks when the beater is lifted straight up.

With a wire whisk, beat about a cup of the whites vigorously into the soufflé base. Then, using a rubber spatula, reverse the process and scrape the soufflé base over the remaining whites. Gently combine them, using the spatula to cut and fold the mixture as you rotate the bowl. Fold gently just until no streaks of egg white show.

Baking the soufflé. Pour the reserved lobster meat–and–sauce mixture into the prepared soufflé dish, distributing the pieces of lobster evenly over the bottom. Pour in the soufflé mixture over the lobster, and smooth the surface with the rubber spatula.

Place the soufflé in the center of the hot baking sheet in the preheated oven and bake for about 30 minutes, or until the top has puffed above the dish and browned lightly.

Finishing the lobster sauce. About 5 minutes before the soufflé is ready to come out of the oven, bring the reserved lobster sauce to a boil over moderate heat. Add the heavy cream and 2 tablespoons of Cognac and, stirring constantly with a whisk, bring the sauce back almost to a boil. Pour it into a heated sauceboat.

Serving the soufflé. As soon as the soufflé is done, rush it to the table. When serving, plunge the spoon to the very bottom of the dish so that each serving will contain some of the lobster. Pass the lobster sauce.

ONION SOUFFLÉ WITH SWEDISH MEATBALLS AND CREAM SAUCE

This is a superb entrée as given here, but you can, if you prefer, make the onion soufflé and the Swedish meatballs separately. If you serve the onion soufflé alone—it is excellent with roast beef, steak, lamb, or chicken—choose a 1-quart soufflé dish and use only 5 whole eggs instead of 6; otherwise follow the instructions exactly.

As for the meatballs alone, prepare as the recipe directs and serve them in the cream sauce as they do in Sweden, accompanied by boiled potatoes; cucumber salad dressed with white vinegar, salt, and pepper; and lingonberries (which are available in jars in stores specializing in Scandinavian foods). You can substitute cranberries, if you like, which have a similar flavor.

SERVES 6

For Preparing the Soufflé Dish
1 tablespoon butter, softened at room temperature
2 tablespoons freshly grated Parmesan cheese

The Swedish Meatballs
6 tablespoons butter, cut into bits
½ cup finely chopped yellow onion (about ½ medium onion)
2 to 3 tablespoons cold water
1½ slices firm white bread, finely crumbled or ground in an
   electric blender or food processor
½ cup milk
1 egg, slightly beaten
1½ tablespoons cornstarch
1 teaspoon salt
⅛ teaspoon freshly ground black pepper
¾ pound mixed beef chuck and lean pork, ground twice
2 tablespoons chopped fresh parsley

The Soufflé Mixture
1 cup coarsely chopped yellow onion (about 1 large onion)
1 cup milk
¾ teaspoon salt
⅛ teaspoon freshly ground white pepper
4 tablespoons butter, cut into bits
4 tablespoons flour
6 egg yolks
9 egg whites
⅛ teaspoon cream of tartar

The Cream Sauce
2 tablespoons meatball drippings or melted butter
1 tablespoon flour
1 cup half-and-half (or more)
Salt
Freshly ground white pepper

Preparing the soufflé dish. Butter a 2-quart soufflé dish with 1
tablespoon of softened butter. Then coat the inside surfaces evenly
with the Parmesan cheese. Refrigerate the dish for at least 30
minutes.
Making the Swedish meatballs. In a heavy 10- or 12-inch frying
pan heat 2 tablespoons of the butter bits over moderate heat until
they froth. Add ½ cup of finely chopped onion and 2 tablespoons
of the water, and stir the mixture with a fork. Cook until all the
water has boiled away and the onion is soft and transparent—
about 5 minutes. If necessary, add the remaining tablespoon of
water to keep the onion from cooking dry before it is soft.

While the onion is cooking, in a large mixing bowl combine the crumbled bread, ½ cup of milk, the slightly beaten egg, cornstarch, 1 teaspoon of salt, and the freshly ground black pepper. This is most easily done with your hands, but you may use a wooden spoon if you like. Add the ground meat and mix all the ingredients together with your hands.

When the onion is tender, add it to the meat mixture and mix it in thoroughly. Set the frying pan aside to use when you fry the meatballs; there is no need to wash it first.

Before shaping the meatballs, place a bowl of cold water on your work surface and line a pan with wax paper. Using a tablespoon dipped into the cold water, shape the meat mixture into 24 balls about the size of walnuts. If the meatballs are not as shapely as you might like, dampen your hands with water and roll the balls again. As you work, place the meatballs on the paper-lined pan. **Frying the meatballs.** Line a second pan with a double thickness of paper towels to drain the meatballs once they have been fried. Add the remaining 4 tablespoons of butter bits to the frying pan in which you cooked the onion, and place it over moderate heat. When the butter begins to froth, add all the meatballs. Shaking the pan constantly to keep the balls turning, cook for about 8 minutes, or until the meatballs are lightly browned on all sides. With a slotted spoon lift them onto the paper-lined pan to drain. Set the frying pan and the meat drippings aside to use in the cream sauce. **Preheating the oven.** Slide an oven shelf into a center slot, place a baking sheet in the center of it, and preheat the oven at 400° F. for 15 minutes.

Making the soufflé base. In a heavy 2-quart saucepan, combine 1 cup of coarsely chopped onion, 1 cup of milk, ½ teaspoon of the salt, and ⅛ teaspoon of freshly ground white pepper. Place the pan over moderate heat and bring the mixture to a boil. Immediately lower the heat and simmer, uncovered, for 10 minutes, or until the onion is tender. Pour the mixture into the container of a blender or food processor, and purée at high speed until it is fairly smooth. Set the onion-milk mixture aside.

Rinse and dry the saucepan. In it place 4 tablespoons of butter bits and set the pan over low heat. When the butter has melted but not browned, remove the pan from the heat. Add 4 tablespoons of flour and stir vigorously with a wooden spoon until the mixture—the roux—is smooth. Then pour in the onion-milk mixture. With a whisk, beat the milk and roux together until they are fairly well combined.

Set the pan over high heat and, whisking constantly, bring

the sauce to a boil. When it is thick and smooth, lower the heat and, stirring frequently, cook slowly for 1 or 2 minutes. Remove the pan from the heat.

One at a time whisk the egg yolks into the sauce. Set the soufflé base aside.

Making the soufflé. Put the egg whites in the bowl of your electric mixer or, if you are using a rotary beater or a large whisk, in a large glass, stainless-steel, or copper bowl. Add the remaining ¼ teaspoon of salt and the cream of tartar. Beat the egg whites until they hold firm, glossy peaks when the beater is lifted straight up.

With a wire whisk, beat about a cup of the whites vigorously into the soufflé base. Then, using a rubber spatula, reverse the process and scrape the soufflé base over the remaining whites. Gently combine them, using the spatula to cut and fold the mixture as you rotate the bowl. Fold gently just until no streaks of egg white show.

Filling the soufflé dish. Place 12 of the meatballs in the bottom of the prepared soufflé dish, leaving a little space between each. Sprinkle with 1 tablespoon of the chopped parsley. Add half of the soufflé mixture, smoothing the surface with a rubber spatula. Carefully arrange the remaining 12 meatballs on top, leaving a little space between each, and sprinkle them with the remaining tablespoon of parsley. Pour the remaining soufflé mixture over the meatballs and smooth the surface with the spatula.

Baking the soufflé. Place the soufflé dish in the center of the hot baking sheet in the oven. Reduce the heat immediately to 375° F. and bake for 30 to 35 minutes, or until the top has browned lightly and the soufflé has puffed.

Making the cream sauce. This is best done while the soufflé is baking. Discard all but 2 tablespoons of drippings from the frying pan or, if you prefer, discard all the drippings and substitute 2 tablespoons of melted butter. Blend in 1 tablespoon of flour, and set the pan over moderate heat. Stirring constantly, cook the mixture for 2 minutes. Remove the pan from the heat and pour in 1 cup of half-and-half and whisk until fairly well combined. Set the pan over high heat and, whisking constantly, bring the sauce to a boil. Reduce the heat and simmer, stirring constantly, for about 5 minutes, or until the sauce has thickened. Taste for seasoning; the sauce may need both salt and pepper. If the sauce has thickened too much, add enough additional half-and-half to bring it to the consistency of a light sauce.

Set the sauce aside until the soufflé is done, reheating it, if necessary, just before serving.

Serving the soufflé. As soon as the soufflé is done, serve it at once, accompanied by the cream sauce in a heated sauceboat.

FRENCH TOMATO AND MACARONI SOUFFLÉ

The tomato soufflé made with a purée of fresh, ripe tomatoes is a classic. But since tomatoes are especially compatible with macaroni, this recipe combines the two. Rather than mix the cooked macaroni into the tomato base, it is more interesting and, possibly, original to layer the macaroni into the tomato soufflé. The result is an excellent luncheon entrée.

SERVES 4

For Preparing the Soufflé Dish
1 tablespoon butter, softened at room temperature
2 tablespoons freshly grated Parmesan cheese

The Tomato Mixture
6 medium-size ripe tomatoes, quartered
¼ cup chopped yellow onion (1 small onion)
1 large clove garlic, peeled and crushed
½ teaspoon sugar
½ teaspoon finely cut fresh basil or ¼ teaspoon crumbled dried basil
1½ teaspoons salt
Freshly ground black pepper

The Macaroni
2 teaspoons salt
2 quarts water
½ cup uncooked elbow macaroni
½ cup freshly grated Parmesan cheese

The Soufflé Mixture
3 tablespoons butter, cut into bits
4 tablespoons flour
6 egg yolks
8 egg whites
¼ teaspoon cream of tartar

The Topping
1 tablespoon freshly grated Parmesan cheese

Preparing the soufflé dish. Butter a 2-quart soufflé dish with 1 tablespoon of softened butter. Then coat the inside surfaces evenly with 2 tablespoons of grated Parmesan cheese and refrigerate the dish for at least 30 minutes.

Making the tomato mixture. In a heavy medium-size saucepan combine the tomatoes, onion, garlic, sugar, basil, 1 teaspoon of the salt, and several grindings of pepper. Set the pan over high heat and bring to a boil, then reduce the heat to low and simmer, uncovered, for 10 to 12 minutes, or until the tomatoes and onions are soft.

Place a food mill over a bowl and pour in the tomato mixture. Process the tomatoes, scraping any of the purée on the underside of the mill into the bowl with a rubber spatula. Return the purée to the saucepan and set it over high heat. Bring the purée to a boil, then lower the heat and simmer, uncovered, for about 10 minutes, or until the purée has reduced to about 1¾ cups. Set the saucepan aside.

Cooking the macaroni. While the tomatoes are cooking, in a large pot add 2 teaspoons of salt to 2 quarts of water and bring to a boil. Add the macaroni to the boiling water and cook, uncovered, for 8 to 10 minutes, or just until the macaroni is tender. Drain the macaroni in a colander or large sieve and set it aside.

Preheating the oven. Slide an oven shelf into a center slot, place a baking sheet on the shelf, and preheat the oven at 400° F. for 15 minutes.

Making the soufflé base. Place 3 tablespoons of butter bits in a heavy 2-quart saucepan over moderate heat. When the butter foams, stir in the flour and cook, stirring constantly, for 2 to 3 minutes. Remove from the heat and whisk in the tomato purée until the mixture is smooth, then set it aside to cool slightly.

Place the egg yolks in a medium-size bowl and, using a wire whisk, beat them until well mixed. Then gradually pour the yolks into the cooled tomato mixture, beating hard with the whisk to combine the ingredients.

Making the soufflé. Put the egg whites in the bowl of your electric mixer or, if you are using a rotary beater or large whisk, in a large glass, stainless-steel, or copper bowl. Add the remaining ½ teaspoon of salt and the cream of tartar. Beat the egg whites until they hold firm, glossy peaks when the beater is lifted straight up.

With a wire whisk, beat about a cup of the whites vigorously into the soufflé base. Then, using a rubber spatula, reverse the process and scrape the soufflé base over the remaining whites. Gently combine them, using the spatula to cut and fold the mixture as you rotate the bowl. Fold gently just until no streaks of egg white show.

Filling the soufflé dish. Mix ½ cup of grated Parmesan cheese with the cooked macaroni; this is most easily done with your hands. Spoon half of the macaroni in a single layer over the bottom of the prepared soufflé dish. Over it pour in half of the soufflé mixture, smoothing it lightly with a rubber spatula. Scatter the remaining macaroni on top and, finally, add the remaining soufflé mixture, again smoothing the surface with a rubber spatula. Sprinkle 1 tablespoon of freshly grated Parmesan cheese over the top.

Baking and serving the soufflé. Place the soufflé dish in the center of the hot baking sheet in the preheated oven. Immediately turn the heat down to 375° F. and bake for 30 to 35 minutes, or until the soufflé has puffed and browned lightly on top. Serve at once.

POTATO SOUFFLÉ WITH GARLIC

SERVES 4

For Preparing the Soufflé Dish
1 tablespoon butter, softened at room temperature
2 tablespoons freshly grated Parmesan cheese

The Potatoes
1½ pounds baking potatoes (about 3 medium potatoes), all
    about the same size
2½ quarts water
2 teaspoons salt

The Soufflé Mixture
2 cups water
2 heads garlic (25 to 30 cloves), separated but not peeled
4 tablespoons butter, cut into bits
2 tablespoons flour
1 cup milk
⅝ teaspoon salt
¼ teaspoon freshly ground white pepper
3 egg yolks
4 egg whites
⅛ teaspoon cream of tartar
3 tablespoons finely chopped parsley (optional)

The Topping
1 tablespoon freshly grated Parmesan cheese

Preparing the soufflé dish. Butter a 1½-quart soufflé dish with 1
tablespoon of softened butter. Then coat the inside surfaces with
2 tablespoons of freshly grated Parmesan cheese and refrigerate
the dish for at least 30 minutes.
Preparing the potatoes. If you are going to mash the potatoes with
a potato ricer, you can boil them with their skins on because the
skins will be entrapped within the ricer; simply scrub them with
a stiff brush under running water. But if you are going to use a
food mill, a potato masher, or a fork, peel the potatoes before
cooking.

Boiling the potatoes. Pour 2½ quarts of water into a 4-quart saucepan, add 2 teaspoons of salt, and bring to a full boil over high heat.

Drop in the scrubbed or peeled potatoes and boil them for 20 to 30 minutes, the exact time depending on their size. At the end of 20 minutes, test them for doneness by piercing the center of a potato with a long skewer. If it meets any resistance, boil the potatoes just until the point of the skewer goes through easily.

Immediately drain the potatoes in a colander and set them aside.

Cooking the garlic. While the potatoes are boiling, you may cook the garlic. Pour 2 cups of water into a small saucepan and bring it to a boil. Add the garlic cloves and boil, uncovered, for 3 minutes over high heat. Drain through a sieve, then cool under running water. When cool enough to handle, peel the garlic cloves by cutting off the root ends with a small sharp knife, then slipping off the skins.

Place 4 tablespoons of butter bits in the top of a double boiler that is set over simmering water, and add the peeled garlic cloves. Cover, set the double boiler over low heat, and let the garlic cloves simmer about 25 minutes, or until they are soft enough to be pierced with a knife.

Mashing the potatoes. Cut the potatoes into quarters, fill the potato ricer with as many quarters as it will hold, and force the pulp into the saucepan in which the potatoes were cooked. Then, with a spoon, remove the peel adhering to the interior of the ricer and continue puréeing the potatoes.

If you are not using a ricer, force the potato quarters through a food mill into the saucepan in which they were cooked, or put the boiled potato quarters directly into the saucepan and mash with a potato masher or a fork.

Set the saucepan of mashed potatoes aside.

Preheating the oven. Slide an oven shelf into a center slot, place a baking sheet on it, and preheat the oven at 375° F. for 15 minutes.

Making the soufflé base. When the garlic is cooked, set the top of the double boiler on a counter; you will no longer need the bottom section of the double boiler.

With a wire whisk, whip the flour into the garlic-butter mixture. Place the top of the double boiler directly over moderate heat and, stirring constantly, cook for 2 minutes; do not allow the mixture to brown. Remove the pan from the heat.

Pour in the milk, add ½ teaspoon of the salt and the white pepper, and mix thoroughly.

Pour the mixture into the container of an electric blender or food processor and purée at high speed until the mixture is smooth; it will be quite thick. At this point taste for seasoning; you may find that it needs extra salt.

Pour the sauce back into the top of the double boiler and set it directly over moderate heat. Whip constantly with a wire whisk until the mixture comes to a boil and thickens, about 2 minutes. Pour the thickened sauce over the potatoes in the saucepan and whip them together thoroughly. The potato-garlic mixture will be very thick and the mixing will require a good deal of effort.

One at a time, beat in the egg yolks. Set the saucepan aside. **Making the soufflé.** Put the egg whites in the bowl of your electric mixer or, if you are using a rotary beater or a large whisk, in a large glass, stainless-steel, or copper bowl. Add ⅛ teaspoon of salt and the cream of tartar. Beat the egg whites until they hold firm, glossy peaks when the beater is lifted straight up.

With a wire whisk, beat about a cup of the whites vigorously into the soufflé base. Then, using a rubber spatula, reverse the process and scrape the soufflé base over the remaining whites. Gently combine them, using the spatula to cut and fold the mixture as you rotate the bowl. Fold gently just until no streaks of egg white show. If you like, scatter the chopped parsley on top and fold in the same way.

Baking and serving the soufflé. Scrape the soufflé mixture into the prepared dish. Smooth the surface with a rubber spatula, and sprinkle the top with 1 tablespoon of grated Parmesan cheese.

Bake the soufflé on the heated baking sheet for 40 to 45 minutes, or until the soufflé is puffed and golden. Serve immediately as an accompaniment to meat.

SPINACH SOUFFLÉ WITH CROUTONS

SERVES 2 TO 4

For Preparing the Soufflé Dish
1 tablespoon butter, softened at room temperature
2 tablespoons fine dry bread crumbs

The Croutons
2 slices firm white bread
3 tablespoons butter, cut into bits

The Spinach Mixture
½ pound fresh spinach
2 tablespoons butter, cut into bits
1 clove garlic, peeled and minced
⅛ teaspoon freshly grated nutmeg
¼ teaspoon salt
Freshly ground black pepper

The Soufflé Mixture
3 tablespoons butter, cut into bits
3 tablespoons flour
1 cup milk
⅝ teaspoon salt
Freshly ground black pepper
5 egg whites
¼ teaspoon cream of tartar

Preparing the soufflé dish. Butter a 1-quart soufflé dish or charlotte mold with 1 tablespoon of softened butter. Then coat the inside surfaces evenly with the bread crumbs and refrigerate the dish for at least 30 minutes.

Making the croutons. Line a jelly-roll pan with a double thickness of paper towels. Cut the crusts off the bread, then cut the slices into ½-inch cubes. You should have about 1 cup of bread cubes.

In a heavy 8-inch frying pan, melt 3 tablespoons of butter bits over moderate heat. Add the bread cubes, tossing them with a wooden spoon until all the butter is absorbed. Then fry the croutons, shaking the pan constantly, until they are golden on all sides. Lift the croutons from the pan with a slotted spoon or spatula and transfer them to the paper-lined pan to drain.

Preparing the spinach mixture. Fold the leaves of spinach, a few at a time and undersides up, in one hand. With the other hand, rip out the stems and discard. Place the spinach in a large bowl of cold water, and stir the leaves gently to dislodge any sand. Drain in a colander, then dry thoroughly in a fresh dish towel or in paper towels. Using a sharp chef's knife, chop the spinach very fine. When chopped, it should measure about 1 cup, firmly packed.

Put 2 tablespoons of butter bits in a heavy 1- or 2-quart saucepan and set the pan over high heat. Heat the butter until it turns a dark brown, almost black; this is important for flavor. Reduce the heat, add the spinach and the garlic, and stir with a wooden spoon until the spinach has absorbed the butter. Add the nutmeg, ¼ teaspoon of salt, and several grindings of pepper. Stir only long enough to mix the ingredients, then cover and cook about 4 minutes. You will notice that the spinach has reduced somewhat in volume. Set the pan aside.

Preheating the oven. Slide an oven shelf into a center slot, place a baking sheet on it, and preheat the oven at 400° F. for 15 minutes.

Making the soufflé base. Place 3 tablespoons of butter bits in a heavy 1½- or 2-quart saucepan and set the pan over low heat. When the butter has melted but not browned, remove the pan from the heat. Add the flour and stir vigorously with a wooden spoon until the mixture—the roux—is smooth. Then pour in the milk. With a whisk, beat the milk and roux together until they are fairly well combined.

Set the pan over high heat and, whisking constantly, bring the sauce to a boil. When it is thick and smooth, lower the heat and, stirring frequently, cook slowly for 1 or 2 minutes. Remove the pan from the heat. Stir in ½ teaspoon of the salt and several twists of the pepper mill.

With a rubber spatula, scrape the spinach mixture into the soufflé base and mix thoroughly. At this point, taste for seasoning; you may find that the mixture needs more salt or even pepper. Set the soufflé base aside.

Making the soufflé. Put the egg whites in the bowl of your electric mixer or, if you are using a rotary beater, in a large glass, stainless-steel, or copper bowl. Add the remaining ⅛ teaspoon of salt and the cream of tartar. Beat the egg whites until they hold firm, glossy peaks when the beater is lifted straight up.

With a wire whisk, beat about a cup of the whites vigorously into the soufflé base. Then, using a rubber spatula, reverse the process and scrape the soufflé base over the remaining whites. Scatter the croutons in and gently combine all the ingredients, using the spatula to cut and fold the mixture as you rotate the bowl. Fold gently just until no streaks of egg white show.

Baking and serving the soufflé. Pour the soufflé mixture into the prepared dish and smooth the top with a rubber spatula. Place the dish on the hot baking sheet in the oven and bake the soufflé for 25 to 30 minutes, or until it has puffed and the top has browned lightly. Serve it at once.

MUSHROOM SOUFFLÉ

SERVES 4

For Preparing the Soufflé Dish
1 tablespoon butter, softened at room temperature
2 tablespoons fine dry bread crumbs

The Mushroom Mixture
½ pound firm button mushrooms
3 tablespoons butter, cut into bits
¼ cup finely diced scallions, white part only

The Soufflé Mixture
3 tablespoons butter, cut into bits
3 tablespoons flour
½ cup homemade or canned chicken broth
½ cup light cream
⅝ teaspoon salt
Freshly ground white pepper
¼ teaspoon freshly grated nutmeg
4 egg yolks
6 egg whites
⅛ teaspoon cream of tartar

Preparing the soufflé dish. Butter a 1½-quart soufflé dish with 1 tablespoon of softened butter. Then coat the inside surfaces evenly with the bread crumbs and refrigerate the dish for at least 30 minutes.

Preparing the mushroom mixture. Wipe the mushrooms with a clean damp cloth. Then, using a heavy French knife, chop them as fine as possible. Place the chopped mushrooms, a handful at a time, in a clean dish towel and twist over a small bowl to extract as much juice as possible. Reserve both the juice and the mushrooms.

In a heavy 8- or 10-inch frying pan, preferably with a non-stick surface, melt 3 tablespoons of butter bits. When the butter foams, add the mushrooms and scallions and stir with a wooden spoon until all the butter has been absorbed. Reduce the heat to very low and cook, uncovered, for 15 to 20 minutes, stirring occasionally, until the mushrooms are dry and have separated and browned noticeably. Remove from the heat and set aside.

Preheating the oven. Slide an oven shelf into a center slot, place a baking sheet on it, and preheat the oven at 400° F. for 15 minutes.

Making the soufflé base. Place 3 tablespoons of butter bits in a heavy 2-quart saucepan and set the pan over moderate heat. When the butter has melted but not browned, add the flour and mix well, using a wire whisk or a wooden spoon. Lower the heat and, stirring constantly, cook the mixture—the roux—slowly until the butter and flour froth without browning—about 3 minutes.

Remove the pan from the heat and stir in the reserved mushroom juice, the chicken broth, and the cream. Return the pan to moderate heat and, beating vigorously with a whisk, cook the mixture until it has thickened. Add ½ teaspoon of the salt, a few grindings of white pepper, and the nutmeg, and stir the soufflé base while you heat it for another thirty seconds. Remove the pan from the heat.

One at a time whisk in the egg yolks. Then stir in the mushroom mixture and whisk until the sauce is smooth. At this point taste the sauce for seasoning; it may need more salt or even pepper. Remember that a soufflé base should be slightly overseasoned if the soufflé is to have any character when the beaten egg whites are added.

Making the soufflé. Put the egg whites in the bowl of your electric mixer or, if you are using a rotary beater or whisk, in a large glass, stainless-steel, or copper bowl. Add the remaining ⅛ teaspoon of salt and the cream of tartar. Beat the egg whites until they hold firm, glossy peaks when the beater is lifted straight up.

With a wire whisk, beat about a cup of the whites vigorously into the soufflé base. Then, using a rubber spatula, reverse the process and scrape the soufflé base over the remaining whites. Gently combine them, using the spatula to cut and fold the mixture as you rotate the bowl. Fold gently just until no streaks of egg white show.

Baking and serving the soufflé. Pour the soufflé mixture into the prepared dish, smooth the surface with a rubber spatula, and set the dish on the hot baking sheet in the oven. Immediately reduce the heat to 375° F. and bake the soufflé for 25 to 30 minutes, or until the top has puffed and is lightly browned. Serve at once.

INDIVIDUAL CORN SOUFFLÉS

Ramekins are small round earthenware or porcelain molds in which food is cooked and served. Custard cups can be used in place of ramekins, if you like.

SERVES 8

For Preparing the Ramekins
1 to 2 tablespoons butter, softened at room temperature
2 to 3 tablespoons fine dry bread crumbs or finely grated Parmesan cheese

The Soufflé Mixture
1 package (10 ounces) frozen whole-kernel corn, defrosted and thoroughly drained
3 tablespoons butter, cut into bits
2 tablespoons finely minced yellow onion (about ½ small onion)
¼ cup water
3 tablespoons flour
¾ cup milk
4 egg yolks
1¼ teaspoons salt
⅛ teaspoon freshly ground white pepper
⅛ teaspoon cayenne pepper
5 egg whites
⅛ teaspoon cream of tartar

Preparing the ramekins. Butter 8 ramekins or custard cups, each holding about 6 ounces, with 1 to 2 tablespoons of softened butter. Then coat the inside surfaces evenly with the bread crumbs or grated Parmesan cheese. Place the individual soufflé dishes on a baking sheet or jelly-roll pan and refrigerate for at least 30 minutes.

Preheating the oven. Slide an oven shelf into a center slot, place an empty baking sheet on it, and preheat the oven at 400° F. for 15 minutes.

Preparing the soufflé base. When the corn is thoroughly drained (it's best to do this in a sieve), pat the kernels dry on paper toweling. Set the corn aside while you make the soufflé base.

Melt 3 tablespoons of butter bits in a heavy 2-quart saucepan over moderate heat. Add the minced onion and the water, and bring to a boil. Cook, uncovered, for about 5 minutes, or until all the water has boiled away, the onions are soft and transparent, and only butter remains. If the onions are not soft and limp, add more water and boil again.

Remove the pan from the heat and add the flour, stirring vigorously with a wooden spoon until the mixture—the roux—is smooth. Then pour in the milk. With a whisk, beat the milk and roux together until they are fairly well combined.

Set the pan over high heat and, whisking constantly, bring the sauce to a boil. When it is thick and smooth, lower the heat and, still stirring frequently, cook slowly for 2 minutes. Remove the pan from the heat.

One at a time, whisk in the egg yolks, stirring after each addition. Add 1 teaspoon of the salt, the white pepper, cayenne pepper, and the corn, and combine all the ingredients briskly with a rubber spatula.

Making the soufflés. Put the egg whites in the bowl of your electric mixer or, if you are using a rotary beater or a whisk, in a large glass, stainless-steel, or copper bowl. Add the remaining ¼ teaspoon of salt and the cream of tartar. Beat the egg whites until they hold firm, glossy peaks when the beater is lifted straight up.

With a wire whisk, beat about a cup of the whites vigorously into the soufflé base. Then, using a rubber spatula, reverse the process and scrape the soufflé base over the remaining whites. Gently combine them, using the spatula to cut and fold the mixture as you rotate the bowl. Fold gently just until no streaks of egg white show.

Baking and serving the soufflés. Using a large spoon, divide the soufflé mixture among the 8 prepared ramekins or custard cups. Then smooth the tops with a rubber spatula.

Pull the oven shelf forward and transfer the small soufflé dishes to the hot baking sheet in the oven, placing them about an inch apart; they should not touch. Reduce the heat to 375° F. and bake for about 15 minutes, or until the soufflés have puffed and the tops are golden.

As soon as the soufflés are done, set them on small individual plates and serve immediately.

OMELET SOUFFLÉ

Louis Diat, the famous chef of New York's old Ritz, once said, "In country places an omelet soufflé is much more often made than a conventional soufflé, probably because it is more quickly and more easily put together."

Traditionally, the platter used to bake the soufflé is silverplated. However, any table-worthy ovenproof platter with a fairly broad flat rim can be used.

SERVES 4

For Preparing the Platter
1 tablespoon butter, softened at room temperature
2 tablespoons granulated sugar

The Soufflé Mixture
6 egg yolks
1 cup superfine sugar
6 egg whites
⅛ teaspoon salt
⅛ teaspoon cream of tartar
8 to 10 ladyfingers
¼ cup Cognac, Armagnac, or light rum

For Dusting
1 tablespoon confectioners' sugar

Preparing the platter. Butter a 12-by-15-inch ovenproof platter with the softened butter. Then coat the bottom of the platter with the granulated sugar and refrigerate the platter for at least 30 minutes.
Preheating the oven. Slide an oven shelf into a center slot and preheat the oven at 425° F. for 15 minutes.
Making the soufflé. Place the egg yolks in a medium-size mixing

bowl. With a rotary or electric beater, beat them just long enough to mix well. Then gradually add the superfine sugar, beating until the mixture is very thick, pale yellow, and makes "ribbons" when it drops from the raised beater.

Put the egg whites in the bowl of your electric mixer or, if you are using a rotary beater or a whisk, in a large glass, stainless-steel, or copper bowl. Add the salt and cream of tartar. Beat the egg whites until they hold firm, shiny peaks when the beater is lifted straight up.

With a wire whisk, beat about a cup of the whites vigorously into the yolk mixture. Then, using a rubber spatula, reverse the process and pour the yolk mixture over the remaining whites. Gently combine them, using the spatula to cut and fold the mixture as you rotate the bowl. Fold gently just until no streaks of egg white show.

Filling the platter. Spoon about a fourth of the soufflé mixture onto the prepared platter, then smooth it over the bottom with a rubber spatula. Arrange the ladyfingers crosswise on top, leaving ⅛ to ¼ inch between each one. Sprinkle the ladyfingers with the Cognac, Armagnac, or rum.

If you are adept with a pastry tube, set aside about 1 cup of the soufflé mixture to use in decorating the top of the omelet soufflé. Otherwise, pour all of the remaining soufflé mixture on top of the ladyfingers, smoothing it with a rubber spatula. Using a fine sieve or sifter, dust the top with the confectioners' sugar.

Baking and serving the soufflé. Place the platter in the center of the oven shelf and bake for 10 to 12 minutes, or until the soufflé has puffed and the top has colored lightly. Serve immediately, making sure that each person gets at least one ladyfinger.

CHOCOLATE SOUFFLÉ

The density of chocolate that gives chocolate cakes their charm has quite the reverse effect in chocolate soufflés. Although chocolate soufflés look more or less like ordinary dessert soufflés, they seldom, if ever, have the same ephemeral lightness. In fact, chocolate soufflés, even when prepared by experts, are usually woolly, puddinglike affairs, because cocoa butter is the natural enemy of stiffly beaten egg whites, and tends to break them down no matter how gently the chocolate and whites are combined. Since it is the air in the beaten whites that expands when the soufflé is baked and causes it to rise, a chocolate soufflé is almost deflated from the start. This recipe solves that particular problem at least. Serve it with unsweetened whipped cream.

SERVES 4 TO 6

For Preparing the Soufflé Dish
1 tablespoon butter, softened at room temperature
2 tablespoons granulated sugar

The Soufflé Mixture
1 tablespoon cornstarch
½ cup milk
2 tablespoons strong coffee or 1 teaspoon instant coffee dissolved in 2 tablespoons boiling water
1 tablespoon orange-flavored liqueur (Grand Marnier, Curaçao, or Triple Sec)
5 tablespoons granulated sugar
⅓ cup semisweet chocolate bits or 2½ ounces semisweet chocolate, coarsely chopped
1 tablespoon butter, cut into bits
4 egg yolks
6 egg whites
⅛ teaspoon salt
⅛ teaspoon cream of tartar

The Whipped Cream
1 cup heavy cream, well chilled

For Dusting the Soufflé
Confectioners' sugar (about 1 tablespoon)

Preparing the soufflé dish. Butter a 2-quart soufflé dish with 1 tablespoon of softened butter. Then coat the inside surfaces evenly with 2 tablespoons of sugar, and refrigerate the dish for at least 30 minutes.

Preheating the oven. Slide an oven shelf into the lower third of the oven and preheat the oven at 400° F. for 15 minutes.

Making the soufflé base. In a heavy 1-quart saucepan beat the cornstarch into the milk with a small whisk. Set the pan over high heat and, whisking constantly, bring the milk to a boil, taking the pan off the heat occasionally to prevent scorching as the mixture gets thick and pasty.

Stir in the coffee, liqueur, 3 tablespoons of the granulated sugar, the chocolate pieces, and the tablespoon of butter bits. Lower the heat and simmer the mixture slowly, stirring constantly until the chocolate has completely dissolved. Then remove the pan from the heat.

One by one whisk in the egg yolks, then return the pan to low heat and, still whisking constantly, simmer for 2 or 3 minutes until the mixture thickens enough to coat a spoon heavily; do not let the mixture come to a boil. Remove the soufflé base from the heat and set it aside.

At this point you may set the soufflé base aside for several hours. Simply cool it to lukewarm, cover it tightly with plastic wrap, and let it sit at room temperature. When you are ready to proceed with the recipe, you must heat the mixture gently to lukewarm before the egg whites can be folded in.

Making the soufflé. Put the egg whites in the bowl of your electric mixer or, if you are using a rotary beater or a large whisk, in a large glass, stainless-steel, or copper bowl. Add the salt and the cream of tartar. Beat the egg whites until they foam thickly, then sprinkle in the remaining 2 tablespoons of granulated sugar, and continue to beat the egg whites until they hold firm, glossy peaks when the beater is lifted straight up.

With a rubber spatula, vigorously stir 4 heaping tablespoons of the egg whites, a tablespoon at a time, into the lukewarm chocolate soufflé base. When the egg whites are thoroughly absorbed, scrape the soufflé base over the remaining whites. Gently combine them, using the spatula to cut and fold the mixture as you rotate the bowl, bringing the heavier chocolate mass up and over the lighter egg whites. Fold gently until only the barest streaks of egg white show, being careful not to overfold or the soufflé won't rise as it should.

Baking the soufflé. Pour the soufflé mixture into the prepared dish, smooth the surface with a rubber spatula, and set the dish in the lower third of the oven.

Bake the soufflé for 2 minutes, then turn the heat down to 375° F. and bake the soufflé undisturbed for 30 minutes if you prefer the center of the soufflé soft, as I do, or for 40 to 45 minutes, if you like a firmer texture. Either way, the top of the soufflé will have risen at least 2 or 3 inches above the rim of the dish.

Making the whipped cream. About 10 minutes before the soufflé is done, place the heavy cream in a well-chilled medium-size mixing bowl and beat the cream until it stands in soft peaks, using a chilled rotary or electric beater. Spoon the whipped cream into a pretty sauce bowl.

Serving the soufflé. As soon as the soufflé is done, dust the top with confectioners' sugar sprinkled through a sieve, and serve it at once, accompanied by the whipped cream.

SOUFFLÉ STANHOPE WITH SAUCE SABAYON

This might be called a two-in-one soufflé in that it is chocolate on the bottom and vanilla on top, with a layer of kirsch-, Cognac-, or rum-flavored ladyfingers in between separating the two flavors.

Although it is somewhat involved to make, it is spectacular and worth the effort. As is true of most soufflés, this one will be rather soft when you plunge a spoon into it. But because the dish is extremely hot, the soufflé will go on cooking after it comes from the oven. It is important not to overcook it lest the chocolate base be too firm.

SERVES 6

For Preparing the Soufflé Dish
1 tablespoon butter, softened at room temperature
2 tablespoons sugar

The Soufflé Mixture
3 ounces unsweetened or semisweet chocolate, coarsely chopped
4 tablespoons butter, cut into bits
4 tablespoons flour
1½ cups milk
½ cup sugar
4 egg yolks
6 egg whites
1 teaspoon vanilla
¼ teaspoon salt
¼ teaspoon cream of tartar
5 to 6 ladyfingers, split in half lengthwise
2 tablespoons kirsch, Cognac, or dark rum

The Topping
2 teaspoons sugar

The Sauce Sabayon
2 egg yolks
1 egg
⅔ cup sugar
¾ cup white wine (dry or sweet)
1 tablespoon kirsch, Cognac, or dark rum (optional)

Preparing the soufflé dish. Butter a 2-quart soufflé dish well with 1 tablespoon of softened butter. Then coat the inside surfaces evenly with 2 tablespoons of sugar, and refrigerate the dish for at least 30 minutes.

Preheating the oven. Slide an oven shelf into a center slot, place a baking sheet on it, and preheat the oven at 375° F. for at least 15 minutes.

Melting the chocolate. Place the chocolate pieces in the top of a double boiler and melt over hot, but not boiling, water. Remove the double boiler from the heat, set the top of the double boiler on a counter, and let the chocolate cool slightly while you make the soufflé base.

Making the soufflé base. Place 4 tablespoons of butter bits in a heavy 2-quart saucepan and set the pan over low heat. When the butter has melted but not browned, remove the pan from the heat. Add the flour and stir vigorously with a wooden spoon until the mixture—the roux—is smooth. Then pour in the milk. With a whisk, beat the milk and roux together until they are fairly well combined.

Set the pan over high heat and, whisking constantly, bring the sauce to a boil. When it is thick and smooth, lower the heat, add ½ cup sugar, and, stirring frequently, cook slowly for 1 or 2 minutes. Remove from the heat and, one at a time, beat in the 4 egg yolks.

Pour half of the soufflé base—about a generous cupful—into a small mixing bowl, and stir in the vanilla. Set this vanilla soufflé base aside.

Beat the melted chocolate into the soufflé base remaining in the sauce, and set the chocolate soufflé base aside.

Making the soufflé. Divide the egg whites in half, placing 3 of them in the bowl of your electric mixer or, if you are using a rotary beater or large whisk, in a large glass, stainless-steel, or copper bowl; place the remaining 3 whites in a second large bowl.

To the first bowl add ⅛ teaspoon of the salt and ⅛ teaspoon of the cream of tartar, and beat the 3 whites until they hold firm, glossy peaks when the beater is lifted straight up.

With a wire whisk, beat about ½ cup of the whites vigorously into the chocolate soufflé base. Then, using a rubber spatula, reverse the process and scrape the chocolate soufflé base over the remaining whites. Gently combine them, using the spatula to cut and fold the mixture as you rotate the bowl. Fold gently just until no streaks of egg white show.

Pour the chocolate mixture into the prepared soufflé dish and over it arrange the ladyfingers, spoke fashion, radiating from the center out. Sprinkle them with the kirsch, Cognac, or dark rum.

To the remaining 3 egg whites in the other bowl, add the remaining ⅛ teaspoon of salt and ⅛ teaspoon of cream of tartar, and beat the whites until they hold firm, glossy peaks when the beater is lifted straight up.

With a wire whisk, beat about ½ cup of the whites vigorously into the vanilla soufflé base. Then, using a rubber spatula, reverse the process and scrape the vanilla soufflé base over the remaining whites. Fold the two mixtures carefully, as above, just until no streaks of white show.

Pour the vanilla soufflé mixture on top of the ladyfingers, and smooth the surface with the rubber spatula. Sprinkle the top with 2 teaspoons of sugar.

Baking the soufflé. Place the dish on the hot baking sheet, and bake for 35 to 40 minutes, or until the soufflé has puffed and browned lightly on top. Serve at once.

Making the sauce sabayon. This sauce, like the soufflé, should be served the instant it is done, so begin making it about 15 minutes before the soufflé is ready to come from the oven.

In the top of a double boiler (not over hot water) beat 2 egg yolks and 1 egg with a wire whisk until they are well mixed. Gradually add ⅔ cup of sugar and continue beating with the whisk or with an electric beater for 5 minutes until the mixture is thick and creamy and makes "ribbons" when dropped from the raised beater. Pour in the white wine and, if you like, 1 tablespoon of kirsch, Cognac, or dark rum. Beat the mixture until smooth.

Set the top of the double boiler over simmering water in the bottom of the double boiler—the top should not touch the water— and cook, whipping constantly with the whisk or beater, until the sauce thickens and doubles in volume—about 7 minutes.

Spoon the hot sauce into a heated serving bowl, and serve immediately with the soufflé.

SOUFFLÉ ROTHSCHILD

Sweet soufflés, such as this one, often use as a soufflé base *crème pâtissière,* a classic cream that is also used as a filling for éclairs, cream puffs, and cakes.

SERVES 6 TO 8

For Preparing the Soufflé Dish
1 tablespoon butter, softened at room temperature
2 tablespoons granulated sugar

The Fruit Mixture
⅔ cup mixed diced candied fruits
¼ cup Cognac or brandy

The Soufflé Mixture
2 cups milk
4 egg yolks
¾ cup granulated sugar
1 teaspoon vanilla
4 tablespoons flour
6 egg whites
⅛ teaspoon salt
⅛ teaspoon cream of tartar

For Dusting the Soufflé
Confectioners' sugar (about 1 tablespoon)

Preparing the soufflé dish. Butter a 1½-quart soufflé dish well with 1 tablespoon of softened butter. Then coat the inside surfaces evenly with 2 tablespoons of granulated sugar. Refrigerate the dish for at least 30 minutes.
Macerating the fruit mixture. Place the candied fruits in a small

bowl, add the Cognac or brandy, and let the mixture macerate for at least 30 minutes while you make the soufflé.

Preheating the oven. Slide an oven shelf into a center slot, place a baking sheet on it, and preheat the oven at 400° F. for 15 minutes.

Making the soufflé base *(crème pâtissière).* Pour the milk into a heavy medium-size saucepan, place over low heat, and slowly bring the milk to a boil.

Meanwhile, in a mixing bowl beat the egg yolks with a wire whisk, rotary beater, or electric mixer just long enough to mix well. Gradually add ¾ cup granulated sugar and the vanilla, and continue beating until the mixture is light, creamy, and makes "ribbons" when it is dropped from a raised beater. Add the flour and mix in just until smooth.

In a slow steady stream pour the hot milk into the yolk mixture, beating constantly. When all the milk has been incorporated, pour the mixture back into the saucepan, set over moderate heat, and cook, stirring constantly with a wooden spoon, until the mixture almost comes to a boil. As you stir, be sure to reach into the crease at the bottom of the pan from time to time. In 5 to 6 minutes, the mixture should be very thick.

Place a fine sieve over a large mixing bowl and pour in the mixture, stirring with a rubber spatula to help it drain through. Scrape into the bowl any of the mixture that clings to the bottom of the sieve. Refrigerate the soufflé base, stirring occasionally until it is cool.

Making the soufflé. Pour the macerated candied fruits into a fine sieve set over a bowl, and let them drain while you beat the egg whites.

Put the egg whites in the bowl of your electric mixer or, if you are using a rotary beater or a large whisk, in a large glass, stainless-steel, or copper bowl. Add the salt and cream of tartar. Beat the egg whites until they hold firm, glossy peaks when the beater is lifted straight up.

Set the sieve with the candied fruits aside, and add the drained Cognac or brandy to the cooled soufflé base (it will probably be lukewarm), and mix in with a rubber spatula.

With a wire whisk, beat about a cup of the whites vigorously into the soufflé base. Then, using a rubber spatula, reverse the process and scrape the soufflé base over the remaining whites. Combine them gently, using the spatula to cut and fold the mixture as you rotate the bowl. Fold gently just until no streaks of egg white show.

Filling the soufflé dish. Pour about a third of the soufflé mixture

into the prepared dish, sprinkle it with half of the candied fruits, then add another third of the soufflé mixture and sprinkle it with the remaining candied fruits. Finally, pour in the last third of the soufflé mixture, and smooth the surface with a rubber spatula.
Baking and serving the soufflé. Place the soufflé on the hot baking sheet, reduce the oven heat to 375° F., and bake for 35 to 40 minutes, or until the soufflé has risen spectacularly and browned lightly.

As soon as the soufflé is done, sift about 1 tablespoon of confectioners' sugar over the top, and serve immediately.

ORANGE PUDDING SOUFFLÉ WITH ORANGE SAUCE

This pudding soufflé is light, moist, and flavorful. It is an extraordinary soufflé in that it can be baked several hours in advance and reheated. The second heating not only makes it puff again, but in no way affects its delicate texture.

SERVES 4

For Preparing the Ring Mold
1 tablespoon butter, softened at room temperature
2 tablespoons sugar

The Pudding Soufflé
3 tablespoons butter, cut into bits
6 tablespoons flour
¾ cup milk
4 egg yolks
3 tablespoons sugar
2 tablespoons strained orange juice
2½ tablespoons chopped orange rind (rind of 1 to 2 oranges)
¼ teaspoon salt
4 egg whites

The Orange Sauce
4 egg yolks
½ cup sugar
½ cup strained orange juice
2 to 4 tablespoons Grand Marnier

Preparing the ring mold. Butter the inside of a 6-cup ring mold thoroughly with 1 tablespoon of softened butter. Then coat the inside surfaces evenly with 2 tablespoons of sugar, and refrigerate the mold for at least 30 minutes.

Preheating the oven. Slide an oven rack into a center slot. Place a roasting pan, at least 3 inches deep, in the center of the rack, and add enough hot water from the tap to half-fill the pan. Preheat the oven and the pan of water at 375° F. while you make the pudding soufflé.

Making the pudding soufflé base. Place 3 tablespoons of butter bits in a small heavy saucepan and set the pan over low heat. When the butter has melted but not browned, remove the pan from the heat. Add the flour and stir vigorously with a wooden spoon until the thick paste—the roux—is smooth. Then pour in the milk and, with a whisk, beat the milk and roux together until they are fairly well combined.

Set the pan over moderate heat and, stirring constantly with a wire whisk, cook until the mixture begins to thicken and comes to a boil; it may be a bit lumpy, but it will smooth out as it cooks. Lower the heat and switch from the whisk to a large wooden spoon, then beat the mixture constantly and continue to cook it slowly until it thickens to an almost doughlike consistency and no longer clings to the bottom and sides of the pan. Transfer it at once to a 2-quart mixing bowl.

While the doughy mixture is still hot, beat in the egg yolks, one at a time, making sure that each yolk is thoroughly incorporated before adding the next. With the wooden spoon, stir in 3 tablespoons of sugar, 2 tablespoons of orange juice, the orange rind, and ⅛ teaspoon of the salt. Set the soufflé base aside.

Making the soufflé. Put the egg whites in the bowl of your electric mixer or, if you are using a rotary beater or a large whisk, in a large glass, stainless-steel, or copper bowl. Add the remaining ⅛ teaspoon of salt, and beat the egg whites until they hold firm, glossy peaks when the beater is lifted straight up.

With a wire whisk, beat about a cup of the whites vigorously into the soufflé base. Then, using a rubber spatula, reverse the process and scrape the orange soufflé base over the remaining whites. Gently combine them, using the spatula to cut and fold the mixture as you rotate the bowl. Fold gently just until no streaks of egg white show.

Baking the pudding soufflé. Spoon—don't pour—the soufflé mixture into the prepared mold and spread the top evenly with the spatula. Don't fill the mold more than three-fourths full or the soufflé will rise too high above the mold and fall over.

With care, pull out the center oven rack and place the mold in the middle of the pan of hot water. If there is not enough water to reach halfway up the mold, add more hot water. Reduce the oven temperature to 350° F. and bake for 40 minutes, or until the soufflé has puffed and filled the mold. (The pudding soufflé will not puff up the way a traditional soufflé does.) To test the doneness of this soufflé, you can insert a cake tester into the side of the risen soufflé; it should come out dry.

Making the orange sauce. While the pudding soufflé is baking, make the sauce. Place 4 egg yolks in the top of a double boiler and beat with a rotary or electric beater just until they are mixed. Gradually add ½ cup of sugar, beating hard until the mixture is pale yellow and creamy. With a rubber spatula, mix in the ½ cup of orange juice.

Place the top of the double boiler over simmering water in the bottom of the double boiler—the top should not touch the water—and cook, stirring constantly with a wooden spoon, until the mixture is thick enough to coat a spoon. Make sure that occasionally you reach into the crease at the bottom of the pan while stirring.

Remove the sauce from the heat and stir in 2 to 4 tablespoons of Grand Marnier, according to your taste. Keep the sauce hot in the top of the double boiler until ready to serve with the pudding soufflé.

Unmolding and serving the pudding soufflé. With care, pull out the oven rack and lift out the pudding soufflé, taking care not to splash it (or yourself) with the hot water around it. Set the mold on the counter and allow it to rest for 5 minutes. Characteristically, the pudding soufflé will have fallen slightly.

Run a small sharp knife around the edge of the mold as well as the center cone. Place a heated serving platter over the mold and, grasping mold and platter firmly with potholders, invert them. The pudding soufflé should fall out easily, particularly if you tap the platter sharply on the counter. Lift the mold off.

Spoon some of the warm orange sauce over the pudding soufflé to coat it lightly. Pour the rest of the sauce into a heated sauceboat and pass it separately.

Reheating the pudding soufflé. If you bake the pudding soufflé ahead, do not unmold it or refrigerate it; simply cover the mold with foil or plastic wrap and let it stand at room temperature. To reheat, preheat the oven and the pan of water to 375° F., as directed above, place the pudding soufflé in the center of the pan of water, lower the oven heat to 350° F., and heat for about 10 minutes, or until the pudding soufflé puffs again (it will not puff quite as much as when first baked). If you want to prevent the top from browning further, cover the mold loosely with a piece of buttered foil. Serve the pudding soufflé with the hot orange sauce as soon as it is done.

SOUFFLÉ CHOCOLATE ROLL

In this admirable creation, popularized by that extraordinary cook Dione Lucas, a chocolate-soufflé mixture is baked on a jelly-roll pan and allowed to collapse and cool. It is then turned out and rolled up, jelly-roll fashion, with a lavish filling of flavored whipped cream. And to intensify its chocolate flavor further (and incidentally camouflage any cracks on its surface), the finished roll is lightly dusted with unsweetened cocoa. Because the chocolate roll contains no flour, its texture, although cakelike, has an aerated lightness few ordinary cakes can approach.

SERVES 8 TO 10

For Preparing the Pan
2 tablespoons butter, softened at room temperature

The Soufflé Mixture

6 ounces semisweet chocolate, coarsely chopped, or 1 6-ounce
  bag semisweet chocolate bits
2 tablespoons strong coffee or 1 teaspoon instant coffee dissolved in 2 tablespoons boiling water
6 egg yolks
½ cup sugar
6 egg whites
¼ teaspoon salt

For Dusting

Unsweetened cocoa (about ⅓ cup)

The Filling

1½ cups heavy cream, chilled
2 teaspoons Cognac or brandy

Preparing the pan. Cut a piece of wax paper to fit exactly the bottom of a 16-by-11-by-½-inch jelly-roll pan. With 1 tablespoon of
softened butter, grease the bottom and sides of the pan, then lay
the wax paper liner into it and, with the remaining tablespoon of
softened butter, grease the wax paper well. Set the pan aside.

Preheating the oven. Slide an oven shelf into a center slot and preheat the oven at 350° F. for 15 minutes.

Making the soufflé base. Place the chocolate pieces and the coffee
in the top of a double boiler and set it over simmering water in
the bottom of the double boiler—the top must not touch the water.
Heat until the chocolate is melted and smooth, stirring well to mix
in the coffee. Lift the double boiler top off the bottom and let the
chocolate mixture cool to lukewarm.

Meanwhile, place the egg yolks in a medium-size bowl. With
a rotary or electric beater, beat the yolks until they are light and
creamy. Gradually add the sugar, beating hard until the mixture
makes "ribbons" and flows thickly off the beater when it is lifted
from the bowl. Slowly beat in the melted chocolate, and continue
to beat until the mixture is smooth and glossy.

Making the soufflé. Put the egg whites in the bowl of your electric
mixer or, if you are using a rotary beater or a large whisk, in a
large glass, stainless-steel, or copper bowl. Add the salt, and beat
the egg whites until they hold firm, glossy peaks when the beater
is lifted straight up.

With a wire whisk, beat about a cup of the whites vigorously into the soufflé base. Then, using a rubber spatula, reverse the process and scrape the soufflé base over the remaining egg whites. Gently combine them, using the spatula to cut and fold and bring the heavier chocolate mixture up and over the lighter whites as you rotate the bowl. Fold gently just until no streaks of white show, being careful not to overfold lest you lose the air you have beaten into the whites.

Baking the chocolate roll. Pour the batter into the prepared pan, spreading it evenly with a rubber spatula. Place the pan in the preheated oven and bake for about 15 to 18 minutes, or until a toothpick or cake tester comes out clean and dry.

As soon as the cake is done, lift the pan from the oven and set it on a cake rack. Wet a clean dish towel or several paper towels in cold water, wring out, and completely cover the top of the cake with the wrung-out toweling. Then cover the wet toweling with a layer of dry toweling, and let the cake cool to room temperature.

Turning the chocolate roll out. When the cake is cool, gently lift off the dry and then the wet toweling—a little of the cake will come away—and run a small knife around the edge of the pan to loosen the sides. Through a fine sieve, sift the cocoa evenly over the top of the cake.

Cut a piece of heavy-duty foil about 2 inches larger than the pan on all sides, and place it over the top of the cake. Then, holding the pan and foil tightly with both hands, invert the pan so that the cake falls onto the foil, cocoa-covered side down and the bottom of the jelly-roll pan facing up.

Place the foil on your work surface, remove the baking pan, and carefully strip off the wax paper liner (which will now be on top). Then, with a sharp knife, cut away any crusty edges.

Filling the chocolate roll. Pour the heavy cream into a chilled, medium-size bowl and beat with a rotary or electric beater until the cream holds a shape. Add the Cognac or brandy, and continue beating until the cream is stiff enough to hold soft peaks. Do not overbeat.

With a rubber spatula, gently spread the whipped cream over the entire surface. If you are adept with a pastry tube, you can reserve about ½ cup of the whipped cream to garnish the sides of the roll with rosettes.

With the long side of the cake parallel to you, use the foil to help roll the cake over on itself. Continue lifting the foil higher and higher with both hands until you have a complete roll with the "seam" on the bottom. The cake will probably crack during the rolling, but don't be concerned. You can sift additional cocoa over the top of the roll to camouflage any serious imperfections.

With scissors or a knife, cut away all the exposed foil along the long sides of the roll, but leave the foil under the roll and at either short end. Using these protruding foil ends as handles, carefully transfer the roll, cradlelike, to a large serving platter or jellyroll board. Cut off all exposed foil and, if you like, finish the roll by piping rosettes of whipped cream around the sides.

Serving the chocolate roll. Try to fill and roll the dessert no more than an hour before serving it so you won't have to refrigerate it, which will stiffen the chocolate and cause the roll to lose its airy texture. If necessary, the roll can be refrigerated for a few hours but not longer, because the cream will "break" and the roll will become soggy.

Serve at table, slicing the roll crosswise into individual portions.

MOUSSES

AND CREAMS

*M*ousses as we now know them can be hot or cold, sweet or savory, and the variations are endless. There are even frozen mousses, often called, mistakenly, iced or frozen soufflés (a true soufflé is cooked, served hot, and reaches its stratospheric heights because of the whipped egg whites folded into the base sauce).

The first mousses must have been sweet. That incomparable chef Escoffier, for instance, described a mousse as an entremets (sweet dish, or dessert) made with cream, gelatin, and innumerable different flavors, such as liqueurs, spirits, coffee, chocolate, fruits, or nuts, which was refrigerated until quite firm.

Cold savory mousses would seem to have been a natural gastronomic progression. Some inspired chef must have realized that if he could combine cream, gelatin, sugar, and puréed apricots, for example, he could also combine cream, gelatin, fish or meat, and suitable seasonings. The next step, apparently, was the creation of the *hot* savory mousse, made with eggs, meat, fish, or vegetables, and cooked in a water bath (bain-marie) in the oven.

There is less confusion over creams, which are elegant desserts that commonly have custard bases. The custard may be plain or flavored, and it may be thickened with gelatin and whipped cream. Sometimes it incorporates whipped egg whites, sometimes fruit. In all its guises, creams are cold and often colorful desserts.

Techniques for Making Mousses and Creams

Preparing the dish or mold. If mousses or creams are to be un-molded for serving, the mold is usually oiled first. With a pastry brush, lightly film the inside of the mold with vegetable oil. Then invert the mold on a double thickness of paper toweling and allow the excess oil to drain off until you are ready to fill the mold.

Some American recipes call for a collar with cold soufflés or mousses to "fake" the height characteristic of a baked soufflé. If you should come across a recipe calling for a collar, this is how you make it: Cut a wide piece of foil, wax paper, or parchment long enough to go completely around the mold and overlap slightly. Then fold the paper two or three times lengthwise, depending on how high you want the soufflé to rise above the mold. Apply the strip of paper to the outside of the mold, pulling it together securely and tightly so that the soufflé mixture can't run down between the paper and the mold. Secure the paper with a piece of string, tying it very tight around the middle of the mold.

Making a custard base. With an electric mixer, rotary beater, or wire whisk, beat the egg yolks with the sugar for 3 or 4 minutes, or until the mixture becomes pale yellow and thick enough, when dropped slowly from a raised beater, to fall back on itself, making "ribbons" that disappear slowly into the mixture.

Slowly bring the milk almost to the boil in a heavy saucepan. Beating slowly, pour the hot milk over the egg mixture in a thin steady stream, and when the ingredients are well combined, pour the mixture back into the saucepan. Cook over moderate heat, stirring constantly and deeply into the sides of the pan with a wooden spoon until the mixture begins to thicken into a light custard that barely coats the spoon. Now lower the heat and continue to cook and stir, raising the pan away from the heat occasionally if it seems to be getting too hot; under no circumstances allow the custard to boil or it will curdle irretrievably. When the custard is thick enough to cling heavily to the spoon, remove it from the heat.

Straining the custard. Many recipes, especially French recipes, call for straining custard after it is cooked. Straining is necessary only if there are lumps or if, by some horrible mischance, the custard has scorched—something that can happen to the best of cooks. To strain, place a fine sieve over a bowl large enough to contain the custard, and pour the custard through; do not force through, particularly if scorched.

Adding gelatin. In very hot and/or humid weather, gelatins tend to take on moisture from the atmosphere. Thus, if the weather is muggy, and if a mousse or cream is to be unmolded successfully so that it will stand on its own, you may need to add an extra 1 teaspoon of unflavored gelatin to the mousse or cream mixture beyond what the recipe calls for.

Cooling a mousse or cream mixture. A quick method of chilling a mousse or custard base is to set a mixing bowl, preferably of stainless steel, into a larger bowl or saucepan that has been filled with a tray or two of ice cubes or crushed ice. Put the mixture to be chilled in the top bowl, and stir with a rubber spatula.

If the mixture contains gelatin, it may thicken and cool sooner than you think—perhaps in 5 minutes or less—and shortly thereafter become a solid gelatinous mass. If that happens, simply reheat the mixture, stirring constantly, until it regains its former consistency.

If you chill the mixture in the refrigerator, which will require more time, stir frequently so that the mixture cools evenly, and if you are going to incorporate other ingredients, keep an eye on it so that it doesn't become too firm.

Whipping cream. Chill the heavy cream, the mixing bowl, preferably of stainless steel, and the beaters well before whipping. For a creamy texture, whip the cream only to the point where it has doubled in volume and barely holds its shape in soft peaks when the beater is lifted from the bowl. Stiffly beaten cream will produce too dense a textured mousse or cream.

Folding in whipped cream. While the custard or other mixture to be incorporated is still fluid but cold and thick, pour it over the whipped cream. Using the flat of a rubber spatula like a shovel, alternately turn the cream over the mixture and the mixture over the cream, occasionally running the edge of the spatula around the sides of the bowl. Continue to fold in this manner until the cream and the mixture are thoroughly combined.

If the mixture to be incorporated has thickened too much, beat in the whipped cream with a whisk instead of trying to fold it in.

If you find that a custard mixture is lumpy after you have folded in the whipped cream, the custard was too firm to begin with. In that case, beat the combined mixture with a rotary beater until the lumps disappear. In fact, if you have any doubts at all about the smoothness of a custard mixture, beat it with a rotary beater.

Improving the color of mousses and creams. The color of certain mousses and creams may not be as clear and pure as you might like. Berries and avocado, for example, when mixed with eggs and cream, may take on a brownish cast. To heighten the color, stick a toothpick into the appropriate food color—red for berries, green for avocado—then stir the toothpick through the mousse or cream mixture. Repeat, bit by bit, until the mixture has taken on a delicate, pleasing color. A dab of yellow coloring, incidentally, usually improves the red hue and the green.

Incorporating egg whites. Generally speaking, most mousses and creams have fewer egg whites than soufflés, and rely less on the aerating power of stiffly beaten whites. In fact, some mousses and creams will be spongy rather than creamy if the whites are beaten too stiffly. To guard against overbeating, you may want to beat whites with a whisk or a rotary beater. Or, if you use an electric mixer, you may want to beat the whites only until they thicken and hold a shape, and then finish beating with a whisk or hand beater.

To fold fragile beaten egg whites into the heavier custard or mousse base, add about a fourth of the beaten egg whites to the base and whip them vigorously with a wire whisk. This lightens the mixture and makes folding easier. Then, using a rubber spatula, scoop the base on top of the remaining egg whites and cut down from the top center of the mixture to the bottom of the bowl. Next, draw the spatula toward you against the edge of the bowl, rotating the bowl as you work. Working quickly, repeat the cutting, folding, and rotating until the whites have been incorporated.

Baking mousses and creams. A hot-water bath (bain-marie) of simmering water helps keep a custard from curdling and provides steady gentle heat for delicate mixtures like mousses. To make your own bain-marie, half-fill a roasting pan with hot water and place on an oven rack to heat while you are preheating the oven. When you are ready to bake the dish, place it in the center of the pan of simmering water. If the water does not reach to about half or two-thirds of the depth of the baking dish, add more hot water.

Unmolding a mousse or cream. If you have prepared the mold or dish properly, you should have no trouble unmolding the mousse or cream. Have your serving platter ready—warmed for a hot mousse, chilled for a cold mousse or cream. Run a knife around the edge of the mold and, if you are using a ring mold, around the center tube as well. Place the serving platter on top of the mold, then, holding both the platter and the mold tightly, invert. If the mousse or cream does not drop out, rap the mold with your hand several times.

If the mousse or cream has not dropped out—and sometimes it won't—wet a towel in very hot water, wring out, and hold it on top of the mold. Usually this works with a recalcitrant mousse or cream, but you may have to apply the hot towel a couple of times. If necessary, you can dip the bottom of the mold in a shallow pan of hot water for 1 or 2 seconds, cover with the serving platter again, and invert.

In the event that the heat has ruffled the surface of the mousse or cream, dip a metal spatula in hot water and smooth out any uneven spots, then return the mousse or cream to the refrigerator for 10 to 15 minutes.

MOUSSE OF SOLE WITH SAUCE BERCY

This dish goes particularly well with small freshly boiled potatoes.

SERVES 6 TO 8

For Preparing the Mold
1 tablespoon butter, softened at room temperature

The Mousse Mixture
1 pound fresh flounder fillets, skinned
5 egg whites
1 teaspoon salt
¼ teaspoon freshly ground white pepper
1¾ cups heavy cream, well chilled

The Sauce Bercy
2 cups (1 pint) clam juice or homemade fish stock
½ cup dry white wine
2 tablespoons chopped shallots or scallion bulbs
2 tablespoons finely chopped fresh parsley
6 tablespoons butter, cut into bits
3 tablespoons flour
Salt
Freshly ground white pepper

Preparing the mold. Butter the inside of a 1½-quart ovenproof mold or soufflé dish with the tablespoon of softened butter, making sure you coat the curve at the bottom of the dish. At the same time, cut a circle of wax paper or foil approximately an inch larger in diameter than the mold and butter one side. Set the mold and the paper aside.

Preheating the oven. Slide an oven shelf into a center slot. Place a roasting pan at least 3 inches deep on the shelf, and add enough hot water from the tap—about 4 quarts—to half-fill the pan. Preheat both the oven and the pan of water at 425° F. for at least 15 minutes, or until you are ready to bake the mousse.

Preparing a "chilling" bowl. Choose a 4- to 5-quart mixing bowl, preferably of stainless steel, and a larger bowl or saucepan into which it will fit. Dump 2 trays of ice cubes into the larger bowl or pan, and place the mixing bowl over the ice to chill.

Making the mousse. Cut the flounder fillets into small pieces. Place half the fish and half of the egg whites in the container of an electric blender or food processor, along with ½ teaspoon of the salt and ⅛ teaspoon of the freshly ground white pepper. Purée at low speed in the blender for about 1 minute, or for 30 to 40 seconds in the food processor, turning the machine on and off, until you have a smooth paste. With a rubber spatula, scrape the mixture into the chilled mixing bowl.

Purée the remaining ½ pound of fish with the rest of the egg whites, and the remaining ½ teaspoon of salt and ⅛ teaspoon of pepper in the same manner. Scrape the purée into the chilled bowl and mix both batches together well.

Stirring hard with a wooden spoon, add the chilled heavy cream very slowly until it is completely absorbed and the mixture has a smooth texture. Taste for seasoning; you may need to add more salt and, perhaps, more pepper.

Baking the mousse. Spoon the mixture into the prepared mold, smooth the surface with a rubber spatula, then cover with the circle of buttered wax paper or foil, buttered side down. Place the mold in the center of the pan of hot water in the oven. The water should reach halfway up the mold; if not, add more hot water.

Bake the mousse for 1 hour. At this point, set the roasting pan with the mold still in it on the counter. The mousse will stay hot for 15 minutes or more.

Making the sauce Bercy. While the mousse is baking, make the sauce.

In a small heavy saucepan, combine the clam juice or fish stock, wine, shallots or scallions, and 1 tablespoon of the parsley. Set the pan over high heat and bring the mixture to a boil, then boil hard until the liquid has reduced to about 2 cups. Remove from the heat and set aside.

Place 3 tablespoons of the butter bits in a heavy 2-quart

saucepan and set the pan over low heat. When the butter has melted but not browned, remove the pan from the heat. Add the flour and stir vigorously with a wooden spoon until the mixture— the roux—is smooth. Then pour in the reduced clam juice or fish stock mixture and, with a whisk, beat the liquid and the roux together until they are fairly well combined.

Set the pan over high heat and, whisking constantly, bring the sauce to a boil. When it is thick and smooth, lower the heat and, stirring frequently, cook slowly for 2 or 3 minutes to rid the sauce of any floury taste. Remove the pan from the heat.

Taste the sauce for seasoning; it may need more salt and pepper.

To finish the sauce, stir in the remaining 3 tablespoons of butter bits and the remaining 1 tablespoon of chopped parsley.

Serving the mousse. Lift the mousse from the pan of water and remove the wax paper or foil. Run a small knife around the edge of the mold, place a heated serving platter on top of the mold, then, holding both the mold and platter firmly, invert them. The mousse should drop out easily.

Spoon some of the hot sauce Bercy over the mousse and pour the remainder into a heated sauceboat. Serve at once.

HAM MOUSSE WITH SOUR CREAM AND HORSERADISH SAUCE

Although the mousse, when turned out from the charlotte mold, is in itself handsome, for an important buffet party, you may want to add a glamorous touch to it by coating the mold with a glistening aspic.

SERVES 6

For Preparing the Mold
1 tablespoon vegetable oil

For Coating the Mold with Aspic (Optional)
2½ cups homemade chicken broth or two 10½-ounce cans chicken broth, thoroughly degreased
1½ envelopes unflavored gelatin
½ cup Madeira

The Mousse Mixture
¼ cup dry white wine
1 envelope unflavored gelatin
1 cup homemade or canned chicken broth, thoroughly degreased
2 cups ground cooked ham, firmly packed
2 tablespoons Madeira
1 teaspoon tomato paste
⅛ teaspoon cayenne pepper
Salt
½ cup heavy cream, well chilled
1 egg white

The Sour Cream and Horseradish Sauce
1 cup sour cream
2 tablespoons prepared horseradish
1 teaspoon prepared mustard

The Garnish
Fresh salad greens
Black and green olives
Sliced tomatoes

Preparing the mold. With a pastry brush, lightly film the inside of a 1-quart charlotte mold with the vegetable oil. Invert on a double thickness of paper toweling to allow any surplus oil to drain off.

If you want an aspic-coated mousse, do not oil the mold. Make the aspic as follows: Pour the 2½ cups or 2 cans of chicken broth into a saucepan, and sprinkle 1½ envelopes of unflavored gelatin over the broth. Place over low heat and stir until the gelatin has dissolved completely, then stir in ½ cup of Madeira. Chill the mixture until syrupy.

Place the charlotte mold in a deep bowl of cracked ice, add the aspic, and swirl around and around until a ⅛-inch-deep layer has set around the edges of the mold; pour out the remaining aspic. If there is too thick a layer at the bottom of the mold, dip a spoon in hot water and scoop out the surplus. Chill the mold until the aspic is firm.

Preparing a "chilling" bowl. Choose a medium-size mixing bowl, preferably of stainless steel, and a larger bowl or saucepan into which it will fit. Dump 1 or 2 trays of ice cubes into the larger bowl or pan, and set both bowls aside, separately, until needed for chilling the mousse mixture.

Making the mousse base. Measure the white wine into a small cup, sprinkle 1 envelope of unflavored gelatin on top, and let soften.

Pour 1 cup of chicken broth into a small saucepan and bring to a boil over moderate heat. Add the softened gelatin and heat, stirring constantly, until the gelatin has dissolved.

Pour the mixture into the container of an electric blender or food processor, add the ground cooked ham, and cover. In the blender process at high speed, and in the food processor use the metal blade and process, turning rapidly on and off, until the mixture is smooth. Using a small rubber spatula, scrape the mixture into the medium-size "chilling" bowl. Add 2 tablespoons of Madeira, the tomato paste, and cayenne pepper, and mix well with a wooden spoon. Taste for seasoning and add salt to taste— the quantity will vary according to the saltiness of the ham. You may also want to add a bit more cayenne pepper.

Making the mousse. Pour the heavy cream into a small chilled bowl and whip with a rotary or electric beater until it is not quite stiff but firm enough to cling to the beater when it is lifted out of the bowl. Set it aside.

Set the bowl of ham mixture in the ice-filled bowl or pan and stir the mixture with a wooden spoon until it begins to thicken and cling to the spoon; this may happen sooner than you think. Then, with a rubber spatula, gently fold in the whipped cream. Remove the bowl from the ice.

Place the egg white in a small bowl and beat with a rotary or electric beater until it holds fairly firm, shiny peaks when the beater is held straight up. Using the rubber spatula, fold it into the mousse mixture, taking care that no streaks of white show.

Pour the mousse into the prepared mold, cover tightly with

plastic wrap, and chill in the refrigerator for at least 2 hours, or until firm.

Making the sauce. Place the sour cream in a small bowl and, with a rubber spatula or wooden spoon, thoroughly mix in the horseradish and mustard. Pour the sauce into a serving bowl, cover tightly with foil or plastic wrap, and refrigerate until you are ready to serve the mousse.

Serving the mousse. To unmold the mousse without aspic, run a sharp knife around the edges of the mousse, place a chilled platter on top of the mold, and invert. If the mousse does not drop out, rap the mold sharply once or twice to loosen and dislodge it.

To unmold the aspic-coated mousse, dip the mold in very hot water for 3 or 4 seconds. Wipe dry. Place a chilled platter on top of the mold and invert. If the mousse does not drop out, give the mold a sharp rap or shake to dislodge it.

Garnish with fresh salad greens, black and green olives, and sliced tomatoes. Serve with the sour cream and horseradish sauce.

INDIVIDUAL CHICKEN MOUSSES WITH SAUCE SUPRÊME

SERVES 8

For Preparing the Ramekins
1 tablespoon butter, softened at room temperature

The Sauce Suprême
2 tablespoons sweet butter, cut into bits
2 tablespoons flour
1 cup homemade or canned chicken broth
¼ cup heavy cream
¼ teaspoon salt
Freshly ground white pepper
½ teaspoon lemon juice

The Mousse Mixture
3 cups diced cooked chicken
3 egg yolks
2 tablespoons dry sherry
½ teaspoon salt
¼ teaspoon freshly ground white pepper
3 egg whites
⅛ teaspoon cream of tartar
1 cup heavy cream, well chilled

The Garnish
A bunch of watercress

Preparing the ramekins. Butter the insides of 8 ramekins or custard cups, each about 6-ounce capacity, with the tablespoon of softened butter, making sure you coat the curves at the bottom. Set aside.

Preheating the oven. Slide an oven shelf into a center slot. Place a roasting pan on the shelf and add an inch or two of hot water to the pan. Preheat the oven and the pan of water at 325° F. for at least 15 minutes.

Preparing the sauce. Place 2 tablespoons of butter bits in a heavy 2-quart saucepan and set the pan over low heat. When the butter has melted but not browned, remove the pan from the heat. Add the flour and stir vigorously with a wooden spoon until the mixture—the roux—is smooth. Then pour in the chicken broth and, with a whisk, beat the broth and roux together until they are fairly well combined.

Set the pan over high heat and, whisking constantly, bring the sauce to a boil. When it is thick and smooth, lower the heat and, stirring frequently, cook slowly for 2 or 3 minutes to rid it of any floury taste. Remove the pan from the heat.

Stir in ¼ cup of heavy cream, ¼ teaspoon of salt, several twists of the pepper mill, and the lemon juice, and whisk until the sauce is smooth. Taste for seasoning, and adjust, if necessary. Cover tightly with plastic wrap, and set aside.

Making the mousse base. Using the finest blade of a food chopper, grind the diced cooked chicken twice, and place it in a large bowl. Or, using the metal blade, process the chicken in a food processor, turning it on and off for 30 to 40 seconds, or until a smooth paste is formed.

Beat the egg yolks with a rotary or electric beater until thick and creamy, and stir them into the chicken paste. With a wooden spoon, add ½ cup of the sauce suprême, the dry sherry, ¼ teaspoon of the salt, and ¼ teaspoon of freshly ground white pepper, and stir all the ingredients until well combined.

Making the mousse. Put the egg whites in the bowl of your electric mixer or, if you are using a rotary beater or a large whisk, in a large glass, stainless-steel, or copper bowl. Add the remaining ¼ teaspoon of salt and the cream of tartar. Beat the egg whites until they hold firm shiny peaks when the beater is lifted straight up. Set aside.

With a rotary or electric beater, whip the heavy cream in a chilled medium-size bowl until it holds a shape; don't overbeat.

With a rubber spatula, fold the beaten whites into the chicken mixture alternately with the whipped cream.

Baking the mousses. Spoon the mousse mixture into the prepared ramekins, dividing it evenly among them. Smooth the tops with a spatula.

Pull out the oven rack and arrange the ramekins in the large roasting pan so that they do not touch one another. The water in the pan should reach halfway up the ramekins; if it doesn't, add more hot water. Carefully and slowly slide the rack back into the oven. Bake for 40 to 50 minutes, or until the point of a knife inserted in the center of one ramekin comes out dry.

When the mousses are baked, pull the rack out as far as is necessary, taking care that no water splashes into the ramekins or on you. Lift the ramekins from the pan and allow to rest for 4 to 5 minutes before unmolding.

Reheating the sauce. While the mousses are resting, reheat the remaining sauce suprême over moderate heat, stirring or whisking it back to its original smoothness.

Serving the mousses. To unmold, run a sharp knife around the edge of each ramekin, then invert on a heated serving platter, leaving a little space between each mousse. Or, unmold each ramekin on an individual heated plate. Spoon the remaining hot sauce over each individual mousse, or serve it separately in a small heated sauceboat. Garnish the platter or each plate with a bouquet of watercress.

COLD SALMON MOUSSE WITH CUCUMBER SAUCE

SERVES 4 TO 6

For Preparing the Mold
2 teaspoons vegetable oil

The Mousse Mixture
1 envelope unflavored gelatin
¼ cup dry white wine
¾ cup homemade or canned chicken broth, thoroughly degreased
2 cups boned, cooked salmon, firmly packed
1 teaspoon paprika
2 teaspoons tomato paste
1 tablespoon finely grated onion
1½ teaspoons salt
1 tablespoon strained fresh lemon juice
⅛ teaspoon Tabasco
½ cup heavy cream, well chilled

The Cucumber Sauce
2 firm cucumbers, each about 6 inches long
1 teaspoon salt
2 teaspoons white wine vinegar
2 cups plain yogurt
2 tablespoons finely chopped fresh dill
¼ teaspoon cayenne pepper

Preparing the mold. Using a pastry brush, lightly film the inside of a 3-cup fish mold or other decorative mold with the vegetable oil. Invert on a double thickness of paper toweling to allow any surplus oil to drain off.

Preparing a "chilling" bowl. Choose a medium-size bowl, preferably of stainless steel, and a larger bowl or saucepan into which it will fit. Dump 1 or 2 trays of ice cubes into the larger bowl, and set both bowls aside, separately, until needed for chilling the mousse mixture.

Making the mousse base. Sprinkle the gelatin over the wine in a small cup and allow it to soften.

Meanwhile, pour the chicken broth into a small saucepan and bring it to a boil. Stir in the softened gelatin with a wooden spoon, and stir over low heat until the gelatin has completely dissolved. Pour into the container of an electric blender or food processor, and add the cooked salmon. Process until the mixture is smooth, in the blender at high speed, and in the food processor using the metal blade and turning on and off rapidly.

With a rubber spatula, scrape the salmon mixture into the "chilling" bowl, and stir in the paprika, tomato paste, grated onion, 1½ teaspoons of salt, lemon juice, and Tabasco. Set aside.

Making the mousse. Pour the heavy cream into a small chilled bowl. Beat, using a rotary or electric beater, until the cream is just firm enough to cling to the beater when it is lifted from the bowl. It should not peak stiffly.

Set the bowl of salmon in the larger ice-filled bowl or pan and stir with a wooden spoon until the mixture begins to stiffen. This happens fairly quickly. Then spoon the softly whipped cream on top of the salmon and fold it in gently but thoroughly with a rubber spatula.

Pour at once into the prepared mold, smooth the surface with a metal spatula, and cover tightly with plastic wrap. Refrigerate for 2 hours, or until firm.

Making the sauce. Using a vegetable peeler, peel the cucumbers, then with a sharp French knife, slice in half lengthwise. Using a teaspoon, scoop out and discard all the seeds and soft pulp from each cucumber half. Chop the cucumbers coarsely, and place them in a small bowl. Stir in 1 teaspoon of salt and the white wine vinegar, and set aside for about 1 hour.

After the cucumbers have marinated for an hour, drain them well and pat them dry on paper toweling. Place them in a medium-size bowl, and thoroughly mix in the yogurt, fresh dill, and cayenne pepper. Taste for seasoning, adding more salt or cayenne, if needed. Cover tightly with plastic wrap and refrigerate until ready to serve.

Serving the mousse. Run a small sharp knife around the mousse, dip the bottom of the mold in hot water for a second or two, and wipe dry with a towel. Place a chilled platter on top of the mold and invert. If the mousse does not drop out of the mold, rap it smartly once or twice to dislodge it. Serve with the cucumber sauce.

AVOCADO MOUSSE WITH MAYONNAISE MOUSSELINE

SERVES 6 TO 8

For Preparing the Mold
1 tablespoon vegetable oil

The Mousse Mixture
1¾ cups homemade or canned chicken broth, thoroughly degreased
2 envelopes unflavored gelatin
⅓ cup coarsely chopped onion (about 1 small onion)
1 teaspoon curry powder
2 tablespoons cider vinegar
2 large ripe avocados
3 to 4 tablespoons strained fresh lime juice
½ cup thick mayonnaise, preferably homemade
1 teaspoon salt
½ cup finely chopped green pepper (about 1 small pepper)
12 to 14 small pimiento-stuffed olives

The Mayonnaise Mousseline
1 egg white
½ cup mayonnaise, preferably homemade

The Garnish
Cherry tomatoes
Pimiento-stuffed olives
Bouquets of parsley or watercress

Preparing the mold. With a pastry brush, lightly film the inside of a 4- to 5-cup ring mold with the vegetable oil. Then turn the mold upside down on paper toweling to allow any excess oil to drain off.

Making the mousse. Pour 1 cup of the chicken broth into a small saucepan, sprinkle the gelatin over the broth, and let soften. Place the saucepan over moderate heat and, stirring constantly with a wire whisk, bring the broth to a boil. Continue to stir until the gelatin has completely dissolved—about 2 minutes. Remove from the heat and set aside.

Pour the remaining ¾ cup of chicken broth into the container of an electric blender or food processor. Add the chopped onion, curry powder, and cider vinegar, and purée until the mixture is absolutely smooth. Pour the purée into the saucepan with the chicken broth–gelatin and mix until well combined. Refrigerate until the mixture has thickened, for at least 20 minutes.

Meanwhile, cut the avocados in half lengthwise. Whack a heavy, sharp knife directly into each seed, then twist and lift out. To peel, place the halves, one at a time, cut side down, in the palm of your hand, and strip off and discard the skin.

Chop the avocados coarsely. Place the avocado pieces in a large fine sieve (or a food mill, if you have one) set over a large mixing bowl, and purée by pressing the avocado through the sieve with a rubber spatula. Scrape any of the purée that clings to the bottom of the sieve into the bowl. Using a wire whisk, blend 3 tablespoons of the lime juice and ½ cup of mayonnaise into the avocado purée.

When the gelatin mixture has thickened sufficiently to coat a spoon, whisk it into the avocado purée until well mixed. Stir in the salt, and taste for seasoning. You may find that the mousse needs more salt, even the extra tablespoon of lime juice. Finally, fold in the green pepper. Set aside.

Filling the mold. Cut 12 to 14 pimiento-stuffed olives in half, crosswise, and place them cut sides down in the bottom of the mold, leaving about ¼ inch between each olive. Ladle the mousse into the mold carefully so as not to disturb the olives, then smooth the surface with a rubber spatula.

Place the mousse in the refrigerator—not the freezer—and allow to set for at least 12 hours, but preferably for 24 hours. The mousse must be firm enough to stand on its own after being unmolded.

Making the mayonnaise mousseline. Make this sauce about 30 minutes before you are ready to serve the mousse.

Place the egg white in a small bowl, then, using a whisk or a rotary or electric beater, beat until it holds fairly firm shiny peaks when the beater is held straight up. Add ½ cup of mayonnaise and beat just long enough to mix well. The final effect will be frothy, reminiscent of whipped cream.

Pour into a serving bowl and refrigerate for at least 10 minutes; chilling helps to firm the sauce.

Unmolding the mousse. Run a sharp knife around the edge of the mold as well as around the center tube. Place a chilled serving platter on top of the mold and, holding both platter and mold tightly, invert. If the mousse does not drop out, rap it sharply with your hand once or twice. If this doesn't work, and sometimes it won't, wring out a towel in very hot water and hold it on top of the mold; you may have to apply the hot towel several times.

If the heat has ruffled the surface of the mousse, dip a metal spatula in hot water and smooth out any uneven spots. Refrigerate the mousse for 10 to 15 minutes before serving.

Serving the mousse. Fill the center of the mousse with cherry tomatoes, and garland the edge with pimiento-stuffed olives and bouquets of parsley or watercress. Pass the mayonnaise mousseline.

CHOCOLATE-ORANGE MOUSSE

A chocolate mousse, in any form, is something else again. Lightness of texture is not crucial to it, and for many tastes, the denser it is, the better. A recipe that has come to be known as a standard chocolate mousse is simplicity itself to make and even easier to remember: four egg yolks beaten into four ounces of hot, melted semisweet chocolate, then four stiffly beaten whites folded in. The mousse may be flavored with chopped candied orange peel or any of the orange liqueurs, for which chocolate seems to have a particular affinity. In this recipe, the orange flavor of the mousse is quite predominant.

However you prepare a mousse, remember that it will be at its best if you let it come almost to room temperature before serving it. Most chilled chocolate desserts suffer a distinct loss of flavor if they are served too cold. A successful mousse may be made with almost any type of cooking chocolate, adding more sugar to the chocolate when necessary.

SERVES 6 TO 8

The Mousse Mixture
4 egg yolks
2 tablespoons sugar
1 tablespoon finely chopped orange peel
6 ounces semisweet chocolate, coarsely chopped
2 tablespoons Grand Marnier
3 tablespoons fresh strained orange juice
8 tablespoons (¼-pound stick) unsalted butter, cut into bits
    and softened at room temperature
4 egg whites

The Garnish (Optional)
½ cup heavy cream, well chilled
Candied violets

Preparing a "chilling" bowl. Choose a medium-size mixing bowl, preferably of stainless steel, and a larger bowl or saucepan into which it will fit. Dump 1 or 2 trays of ice cubes into the larger bowl or pan, and set both bowls aside, separately, until needed for chilling the mousse mixture.

Making the mousse base. In the stainless-steel mixing bowl—the "chilling" bowl—combine the egg yolks and sugar, and beat them with a whisk or rotary or electric beater until they thicken enough to fall back on themselves in a "ribbon" when the mixture is lifted from the bowl. Stir in the chopped orange peel.

Place the bowl in a skillet filled with enough hot water to come to about 2 inches up the sides of the mixing bowl. Place the skillet over low heat—the water must simmer, never boil—and resume beating the egg mixture until it foams thickly and, when tested, feels almost too hot to the touch. This should take about 3 or 4 minutes.

Remove the bowl from the skillet and place it in the larger bowl of ice cubes. Beat for 3 or 4 minutes longer, or until the mixture is cold, thick, and creamy. Set aside.

Place the chocolate pieces in a small saucepan and, stirring constantly with a wooden spoon or a rubber spatula, melt it over low heat. Do not at any time allow it to boil, and watch it carefully, it scorches easily.

Remove the pan from the heat and, with a whisk, beat into it, one tablespoon at a time, the Grand Marnier and then the orange juice. Bit by bit, beat in the softened butter. When the mixture is smooth and glossy, stir it into the cold egg yolk mixture.

Making the mousse. Put the egg whites in a glass, stainless-steel, or, preferably, unlined copper bowl. Beat them with a balloon whisk or rotary beater—not an electric mixer, although an electric hand beater will do—until they foam, then continue beating until they form soft, wavering peaks on the beater when it is lifted from the bowl. The whites must not be too stiffly beaten or the mousse will be spongy rather than creamy.

With a rubber spatula, mix about ½ cup of the whites into the mousse base, then pour the mousse base over the remaining egg whites, and gently but thoroughly fold the two together.

Pour the mousse into a 1-quart soufflé dish, smooth the top with the rubber spatula, and cover tightly with plastic wrap. Refrigerate for at least 6 hours, or until the mousse is fairly firm.

Serving the mousse. If you want to serve the mousse in an especially festive way, whip the cream stiffly in a chilled mixing bowl, and pipe it on top of the mousse in swirls or kisses through a pastry bag fitted with a decorative tip. Decorate the cream with a few candied violets. Or simply serve the whipped cream in a pretty bowl.

ORANGE-PUMPKIN MOUSSE

Long known primarily in pumpkin pie, here is pumpkin in a new guise, spiked with orange juice and garnished with candied orange rind. A dessert worthy of important parties.

As a matter of interest, the candied orange rind makes a beautiful garnish on a frosted chocolate cake or fresh orange sections in syrup. And the same recipe can be used to make candied grapefruit or lemon rind. Once the candied rind is made, store it in a tightly covered container at room temperature.

SERVES 6

For Preparing the Mold
1 tablespoon vegetable oil

The Mousse Mixture
2 egg yolks
¾ cup heavy cream
1 envelope unflavored gelatin
½ cup firmly packed light-brown sugar
½ teaspoon salt
½ teaspoon freshly grated nutmeg
½ teaspoon powdered cinnamon
1-pound can pumpkin meat
½ cup strained fresh orange juice
Grated rind of 1 orange
2 egg whites
¼ cup granulated sugar

The Candied Orange Rind
3 large navel oranges
2 cups granulated sugar
1 cup water

The Garnish
1 cup heavy cream, well chilled

Preparing the mold. With a pastry brush, lightly film the inside of a 6-cup mold with the vegetable oil. Turn the mold upside down on a double thickness of paper toweling to drain off any excess oil. **Making the mousse base.** Put the egg yolks in the top of a double boiler, add ¾ cup of heavy cream, and, off the heat, beat well with a wire whisk. Add the gelatin, light-brown sugar, ¼ teaspoon of the salt, the nutmeg, and the cinnamon, and, with a wooden spoon, stir until well combined.

Place the top of the double boiler over the simmering water in the bottom of the double boiler—the top should not touch the water—and cook, stirring constantly, until the gelatin dissolves, about 6 minutes.

Remove from the heat and pour into a large mixing bowl. Stir in the pumpkin meat, orange juice, and the grated orange rind. Place in the refrigerator and, stirring occasionally, chill until the mixture has cooled and mounds when dropped from a spoon. This will take about 20 or 30 minutes.

Making the mousse. Put the egg whites in the bowl of your electric mixer or, if you are using a rotary beater or a whisk, in a large glass, stainless-steel, or copper bowl. Add the remaining ¼ teaspoon of salt. Beat the whites until they begin to hold a soft shape. Gradually add ¼ cup of granulated sugar and continue beating until the meringue is very stiff and shiny.

Spoon the meringue on top of the chilled pumpkin mixture and, using a rubber spatula, fold in carefully so as not to lose any volume.

Pour the mousse into the prepared mold, smooth the top with the rubber spatula, cover tightly with plastic wrap, and refrigerate until firm. This will take about 8 hours, or overnight.

Making the candied orange rind. With a vegetable peeler, cut the rind off the navel oranges in wide pieces, taking care not to pick up any of the white part of the skin. Then, using a sharp knife, cut the rind into long slivers.

Combine 1 cup of the granulated sugar and the water in a medium-size heavy saucepan. Bring to a boil, add the slivered orange rind, reduce the heat to very low, and cook, uncovered, for about 45 minutes, or until almost all the syrup has disappeared.

Meanwhile, sprinkle the remaining cup of granulated sugar over a large baking sheet. When the rind is cooked, with a kitchen fork, transfer the pieces from the syrup to the sugar-coated baking sheet. Toss the rind with the fork until all pieces are coated with sugar. Set aside to dry before using.

Serving the mousse. When the mousse is well chilled and firm enough to unmold, run a small sharp knife around the edge of the mousse. Place a chilled serving platter on top of the mold, and then, holding the platter and mold firmly, invert. If the mousse does not drop out, rap the mold sharply once or twice to dislodge it.

With a rotary or electric beater, whip the heavy cream in a chilled bowl until it holds a shape. If you are adept with the pastry tube, pipe a few rosettes around the base of the mousse. Otherwise, spoon a few decorative dollops around the base, then garnish the edge of the mousse all around with the candied orange rind. Spoon any remaining whipped cream into a small serving bowl.

APRICOT MOUSSE WITH CRÈME CHANTILLY

SERVES 6 TO 8

The Mousse Mixture
8 ounces (1 bag) dried apricots
2 cups water
3 egg yolks
1¼ cups milk
1 cup sugar
2 envelopes unflavored gelatin
3 tablespoons strained fresh lemon juice
3 egg whites
⅛ teaspoon salt
1 cup heavy cream, well chilled

The Garnish
2 cups Crème Chantilly, page 171

Preparing the apricots. Place the dried apricots in a small saucepan, add the water, and bring to a boil over high heat. Reduce the heat and simmer, uncovered, for 18 to 20 minutes, or until the apricots are tender when pierced with a fork.

Pour the apricots and liquid into the container of an electric blender or food processor. Cover, then turn on and off immediately. You should have a coarse purée—that is, small pieces of the apricot still unblended. If necessary, repeat the quick on-and-off; do not overpurée. Set the apricot mixture aside.

Making the mousse base. Put the egg yolks into the top of a double boiler. Off the heat, beat the yolks lightly with a wire whisk, then stir in the milk. In a small bowl, combine ¾ cup of the sugar and the unflavored gelatin, and stir this into the yolk mixture, beating together until well combined. Place the top of the double boiler over simmering water in the bottom of the double boiler— the top should not touch the water—and cook, beating constantly, until the mixtume thickens slightly, about 5 minutes.

Remove from the heat, and stir in the lemon juice and apricot purée. Mix together thoroughly, cover tightly with plastic wrap, and place in the refrigerator for about 40 minutes, or until cool.

Making the mousse. Place the egg whites in the bowl of your electric mixer or, if you are using a rotary beater or a wire whisk, in a large glass, stainless-steel, or copper bowl. Add the salt, and beat the whites until they begin to hold a shape. Gradually add the remaining ¼ cup of sugar, beating constantly, until the meringue holds firm, shiny peaks when the beater is held straight up. Set aside.

Pour the heavy cream into a medium-size chilled mixing bowl. With the same beater (it isn't necessary to wash it for the cream), whip the cream until it forms soft peaks.

With a wire whisk, beat 4 to 5 tablespoons of the meringue into the apricot mixture. Then, with a rubber spatula, pile the apricot mixture over the remaining meringue, scrape the whipped cream over the apricot mixture, and fold in the whites and whipped cream, using the spatula to cut and fold the mixture as you rotate the bowl. Fold gently but thoroughly until no streaks of white show.

Pour the mousse into a handsome 2-quart serving bowl (crystal would be attractive) and smooth and swirl the surface with the spatula. Cover tightly with plastic wrap or foil and refrigerate for at least 8 hours.

Making the crème Chantilly. About 5 minutes before serving the mousse, make the crème Chantilly according to the recipe that follows. Spoon it into a small serving bowl and pass it separately while you serve the mousse.

CRÈME CHANTILLY

Crème Chantilly, nothing more than sweetened and flavored whipped cream, is a quick and easy way to dress up any cold dessert. Make it just before you are ready to serve the dessert so that the cream won't "break" (separate and lose volume). The whipping takes only a minute.

MAKES 2 CUPS

1 cup heavy cream, well chilled
2 tablespoons sifted confectioners' sugar
1 tablespoon Cognac, brandy, dark rum, Grand Marnier, Cointreau, or other liqueur

Whipping the cream. Place the heavy cream in a well-chilled medium-size mixing bowl. Then, with a chilled rotary or electric hand beater, beat until the cream stands in soft peaks. Gently fold in the confectioners' sugar and the Cognac, brandy, dark rum, or liqueur—whatever will enhance the flavor of the particular dessert it is served with.

Serving the crème Chantilly. Spoon into a small pretty serving bowl and pass. Or, to dress up an unmolded mousse, drop small mounds of crème Chantilly from a teaspoon in a decorative way around the base of the mousse, then garnish with a few mint leaves. Or, if you are adept with the pastry tube, spoon some of the crème Chantilly into a pastry bag fitted with a fluted tube and pipe rosettes around the base of the mousse.

FROZEN MAPLE MOUSSE

SERVES 4 TO 6

4 egg yolks
⅛ teaspoon salt
1 cup pure maple syrup
1 teaspoon vanilla
2 cups heavy cream, well chilled
½ cup finely grated walnuts

Making the mousse base. Place the egg yolks in the top of a double boiler and add the salt. Off the heat, beat the yolks with a rotary or electric hand beater until very thick and creamy. Set aside.

Pour the maple syrup into a small saucepan and cook over moderate heat until the syrup begins to simmer (205° to 210° F. on a candy thermometer). Beating constantly with a wire whisk, add the hot syrup to the yolks in the top of the double boiler in a slow steady stream. This will take about 2 minutes.

Place the mixture over simmering water in the bottom of the double boiler—the top should not touch the water. Beating constantly with the whisk, cook the mixture until it thickens enough to coat a spoon—about 5 minutes. Remove from the heat and stir in the vanilla.

To cool the mixture, place the double boiler top in the refrigerator for about 15 minutes.

Making the mousse. Whip the heavy cream in a well-chilled bowl with a rotary or electric hand beater until the cream holds soft peaks when the beater is lifted from the bowl.

Add about a third of the whipped cream to the cooled mousse base and beat it in vigorously with a wire whisk. Then, using a rubber spatula, reverse the process and scrape the mousse base over the remaining whipped cream. Gently combine them, using the spatula to cut and fold the mixture as you rotate the bowl. Fold in gently but thoroughly until no streaks of white show.

Pour the mousse into a 1-quart charlotte mold or porcelain soufflé dish, and smooth the surface with a rubber spatula. Sprinkle half of the grated walnuts over the top. Set the remaining nuts aside.

Freezing the mousse. Place the mold in the freezer. If your refrigerator does not have a separate freezer maintaining 0° temperature, place the mold in the freezing compartment and turn the dial to the lowest point. Allow at least 8 hours to freeze the mousse; it is extra rich and requires somewhat more time.

Serving the mousse in the mold. The mousse can be served directly from the mold, if you like, in which case, place the mold in the refrigerator about 30 minutes before serving. This will "temper" the mousse, allowing it to soften sufficiently for serving. Just before bringing it to table, sprinkle the remaining grated walnuts on top of the mousse.

Serving the mousse unmolded. Run a small knife around the edge of the mold to loosen the mousse. Then dip the bottom of the mold in a pan of warm water for a few seconds, cover the top of the mold with a well-chilled platter, and invert.

Or, invert the mold on the serving platter and, around the mold, hold a towel wrung out in very hot water. In either case, knock the inverted mold sharply to help release the mousse. Should the surface of the mousse become ruffled during the unmolding, smooth it with a metal spatula. And if the mousse softens too much during the unmolding, simply return it to the freezer briefly.

When the mousse is unmolded on the platter, sprinkle it with the remaining grated walnuts. To serve, cut the mousse as you would a cake.

FROZEN CRANBERRY MOUSSE

SERVES 8

The Mousse Mixture
2 cups heavy cream
2 cups fresh or frozen whole cranberries
1 cup sugar
½ cup water
¾ cup strained fresh orange juice
¼ cup Curaçao or Grand Marnier

The Garnish (Optional)
½ cup heavy cream, well chilled
2 tablespoons chopped candied fruits

Chilling the cream and serving glasses. Pour 2 cups of heavy cream into a large mixing bowl or the bowl of the electric mixer. Place in the refrigerator to chill. At the same time, chill 8 tulip-shaped wineglasses or parfait glasses in the refrigerator.
Making the mousse base. Pick over the cranberries, discarding any that seem to be damaged. Wash them in a colander or sieve under running water, and set them aside to drain.

In a heavy 2-quart saucepan, combine the sugar and water. Place over moderate heat and stir with a wooden spoon until the sugar has dissolved. Then bring to a boil. Add the cranberries, and bring to a boil again. Reduce the heat and simmer, uncovered, for 5 to 10 minutes, or until the cranberries pop, are tender, and the mixture has thickened noticeably.

Set a food mill or medium-size strainer over a mixing bowl large enough to hold the cranberries. Pour in the cooked cranberries. If you are using a strainer, press the mixture through the sieve with a rubber spatula. If using a food mill, turn the mill until all the cranberries have been puréed. With the spatula, scrape any of the purée from the bottom of the sieve or mill into the bowl.

Stir the orange juice and Curaçao or Grand Marnier into the cranberry purée, and mix well. Refrigerate for about 30 minutes.
Making the mousse. With a rotary or electric hand beater, or using

the electric mixer, whip the 2 cups of chilled cream until it forms fairly firm peaks. Do not overbeat or you will have butter.

Pour the chilled cranberry purée over the whipped cream, then, with a rubber spatula, fold in carefully until no white shows. Spoon the mousse into the chilled glasses, smoothing the surfaces with the spatula. Place in the freezer until frozen, about 3 hours. **Serving the mousses.** About 20 minutes before you wish to serve dessert, place the glasses in the refrigerator to "temper"—to soften—the mousse.

If you want to garnish the mousses, just before serving, whip ½ cup of heavy cream in a chilled bowl until it forms soft peaks, then fold in the chopped candied fruits. Spoon a dollop on top of each portion.

PINEAPPLE BAVARIAN CREAM WITH CRÈME CHANTILLY

Bavarois, or *crème Bavarois,* is the same dessert we Americans call Bavarian cream. It can be a plain custard thickened with gelatin and whipped cream, or a custard made with gelatin, whipped cream, and puréed or crushed fruits, as in the two recipes here: Pineapple Bavarian Cream and Strawberry Bavarian Cream.

Although Bavarian creams are generally unmolded before serving, this pineapple version is so delicate and light that it is best to serve it straight from the dish in which it was chilled—in which case, of course, the dish should be attractive enough to go to the table.

The Bavarian Cream
One 20-ounce can crushed pineapple, packed in its own juice
2 envelopes unflavored gelatin
1 cup dark rum
4 egg yolks
¾ cup granulated sugar
2 cups milk
4 egg whites
⅛ teaspoon salt
1 cup heavy cream, well chilled
1 tablespoon confectioners' sugar

The Garnish
2 cups Crème Chantilly, page 171

Preparing the pineapple. Pour the contents of the can of crushed pineapple into a fine sieve set over a medium-size bowl, and allow all the juice to drain off. Stir the pineapple occasionally with a rubber spatula to encourage draining. When thoroughly drained, sprinkle the gelatin over the pineapple juice and set aside to soften.

Transfer the drained, crushed pineapple from the sieve to a medium-size bowl and stir in the rum. Cover and allow the pineapple to macerate in the rum for at least 1 hour.

Set the sieve over a bowl, and again pour the crushed pineapple into the sieve and allow it to drain thoroughly. Set aside both the sieve of crushed pineapple and the bowl of drained rum.
Making the custard base. Put the egg yolks in a medium-size bowl and beat them with a rotary or electric beater until well mixed. Gradually add the granulated sugar, beating hard until the mixture turns pale yellow and thickens enough to make "ribbons" as it falls from the raised beater.

Slowly bring the milk almost to the boil in a medium-size heavy saucepan. Beating slowly, pour the hot milk over the yolk mixture in a thin steady stream, and when the ingredients are well combined, pour the mixture back into the saucepan. Cook over moderate heat, stirring constantly and deeply into the sides of the pan with a wooden spoon until the mixture begins to thicken into a light custard that barely coats the spoon. Now lower the heat and continue to cook and stir, raising the pan away from the heat occasionally if it seems to be getting too hot; under no circumstances allow the custard to boil or it will curdle irretrievably. When the custard is thick enough to cling heavily to the spoon, remove it from the heat and stir in the softened gelatin until it has completely dissolved. Cover tightly with plastic wrap and cool the custard in the refrigerator until it has thickened slightly; it should not be stiff or completely firm. This happens faster than you think, so keep an eye on the custard while it cools. **Adding the egg whites.** Put the egg whites in the bowl of your electric mixer or, if you are using a rotary beater or a large whisk, in a large glass, stainless-steel, or copper bowl. Add the salt, and beat the whites until they hold firm, shiny peaks when the beater is lifted straight up.

With a wire whisk, beat about a cup of the whites vigorously into the cool custard. Then, using a rubber spatula, reverse the process and scrape the custard over the remaining whites. Gently combine them, using the spatula to cut and fold the mixture as you rotate the bowl. Fold gently just until no streaks of egg white show. Refrigerate the mixture until cold and not quite set; it should not be absolutely firm.

Completing the Bavarian cream. When the custard mixture is almost firm, add the reserved crushed pineapple and mix in thoroughly with a rubber spatula. Refrigerate while you whip the cream.

Pour the chilled heavy cream into a chilled bowl and beat with a rotary or electric hand beater until it holds soft peaks when the beater is lifted. Then beat in the confectioners' sugar. Finally, stir in 2 tablespoons of the reserved rum. Taste at this point to see if the cream needs more sugar and/or rum.

Using a rubber spatula, scrape the whipped cream over the custard-pineapple mixture and fold in carefully. Pour the mixture into a 2-quart serving dish, and smooth the surface with the rubber spatula. Cover tightly with plastic wrap or foil, and refrigerate for 6 to 8 hours, or until the Bavarian cream is firm.

Making the crème Chantilly. About 5 minutes before you are ready to serve the Bavarian cream, make the crème Chantilly according to the recipe. Spoon it into a small serving bowl and pass to your guests.

STRAWBERRY BAVARIAN CREAM

This elegant and delicious cream can be made a day or so in advance—kept refrigerated, of course, and tightly covered. Note, however, that the strawberry garnish should never be added until just before serving time because the berries will soften sitting in the cream.

SERVES 8

2 pints fresh ripe strawberries
1¼ cups granulated sugar
2 to 4 tablespoons confectioners' sugar
¼ cup cold water
1 envelope plus 1½ teaspoons unflavored gelatin
6 egg yolks
1½ cups milk
2 teaspoons lemon juice
1½ cups heavy cream, well chilled

Preparing the strawberries. Pour the strawberries into a colander or large strainer, wash under cold running water, then hull. Set aside 10 of the prettiest berries to use as a garnish, then slice all of the remaining berries.

Place half of the sliced berries in a small heavy saucepan. Add ½ cup of the granulated sugar, and mix with your hands. Set aside for 15 minutes so that the juices begin to run.

Place the saucepan of strawberries over moderate heat and simmer, uncovered, for about 10 minutes, or until the berries are soft and the juices have thickened slightly. Place a fine sieve over a bowl and push the cooked berries through the sieve with a wooden spoon or rubber spatula. Set the purée aside.

Place the remaining sliced strawberries in a bowl and sprinkle them with 2 tablespoons of the confectioners' sugar. Set them aside.

Making the custard base. Measure the cold water into a cup and sprinkle the unflavored gelatin over it. Set aside.

Put the egg yolks in a medium-size bowl and beat them with a rotary or electric beater until well mixed. Gradually add the remaining ¾ cup of granulated sugar, beating hard until the mixture turns pale yellow and thickens enough to make "ribbons" as it falls from the raised beater.

Slowly bring the milk almost to the boil in a medium-size heavy saucepan. Beating slowly, pour the hot milk over the yolk mixture in a thin steady stream, and when the ingredients are well combined, pour the mixture back into the saucepan. Cook over moderate heat, stirring constantly and deeply into the sides of the pan with a wooden spoon until the mixture begins to thicken into a light custard that barely coats the spoon. Now lower the heat and continue to cook and stir, raising the pan away from the heat occasionally if it seems to be getting too hot; under no circumstances allow the custard to boil or it will curdle irretrievably. When the custard is thick enough to cling to the spoon heavily, remove it from the heat and stir in the softened gelatin until it has completely dissolved.

Place the saucepan in the refrigerator, and stir occasionally to hasten the cooling. If the custard should thicken too much, beat vigorously with a wire whisk. When cool, stir in the lemon juice and the strawberry purée. Return to the refrigerator until the mixture begins to set—about 5 minutes or so.

Completing the Bavarian cream. Place about half of the remaining sliced strawberries in the container of an electric blender or food processor. Purée for a few seconds, add the remaining sliced berries and all the juices, and process again for a few seconds. The strawberry purée will not be absolutely smooth. Taste here for sweetness; you may want to add some or all of the remaining 2 tablespoons of confectioners' sugar. Take care, however, not to oversweeten the fruit. Set the purée aside.

Pour the heavy cream into a large chilled mixing bowl. Beat with a rotary or electric beater until the cream holds a soft shape, but do not overbeat.

Pour the thickened strawberry-custard mixture over the whipped cream, then, with a rubber spatula, fold in carefully but thoroughly.

Pour the puréed strawberries into the bottom of a 1½-quart serving bowl, preferably glass or crystal. Carefully spoon the Bavarian cream on top of the strawberries. The weight of the custard will displace the purée somewhat, but don't give that a second thought. Smooth the surface of the Bavarian cream with a rubber spatula. Make a tent of foil or plastic wrap to encase the top of the dish completely, then refrigerate for at least 6 to 8 hours, or until the Bavarian cream is firm.

Serving the Bavarian cream. To bring out the full flavor, bring the Bavarian cream to room temperature before serving, and garnish the top with the reserved strawberries, using them either whole (stems down) or sliced.

Since the purée at the bottom of the bowl is really a sauce, plunge your serving spoon deep into the dish so that each serving will include both cream and strawberry "sauce."

CHARLOTTE RUSSE

Originally the charlotte russe was made with apples, later with other fruits, and served hot. Today, it is closely related to Bavarian cream in that it is essentially a cold, liqueur- or vanilla-flavored custard made with gelatin and enriched with eggs and cream. It is molded in the traditional round metal charlotte mold, the walls of which are lined with ladyfingers. It is unmolded for serving and customarily garnished with sweetened whipped cream, although the charlotte itself is so rich that a garnish seems almost unnecessary.

SERVES 8

The Charlotte Russe Mixture
15 to 16 ladyfingers, split in half lengthwise
¼ cup cold water
1 envelope plus 1½ teaspoons unflavored gelatin
6 egg yolks
¾ cup sugar
1½ cups milk
2 to 3 tablespoons Kirsch
1½ cups heavy cream, well chilled

The Garnish (Optional)
1 cup heavy cream, well chilled
Candied violets

Preparing the charlotte mold. Cut off the rounded ends of each ladyfinger half, then trim about half of the split ladyfingers so that they taper to points like daisy petals. Arrange the trimmed ladyfingers, sugared sides down and points toward the center, radiating in a daisy pattern over the bottom of a 1½-quart charlotte mold. In all likelihood, they will not lie perfectly flat, but don't be concerned; however, one end of each ladyfinger should butt against the wall of the mold. When the bottom of the mold is covered, take a 1-inch cookie cutter and cut out, then discard, the tapered ends in the center of the daisy. Next, with the same cutter, cut a round out of one of the remaining split ladyfingers, and place this round in the cutout in the "eye" of the daisy.

Stand the remaining ladyfingers around the wall of the mold, side by side, with the sugared sides against the mold. Set aside while you prepare the custard.

Making the custard base. Measure the cold water into a cup and sprinkle the unflavored gelatin over it. Set aside to soften.

Put the egg yolks in a medium-size bowl and beat them with a rotary or electric beater until well mixed. Gradually add the sugar, beating hard until the mixture turns pale yellow and thickens enough to make "ribbons" as it falls from the raised beater.

Slowly bring the milk almost to the boil in a medium-size heavy saucepan. Beating slowly, pour the hot milk over the yolk mixture in a thin steady stream, and when the ingredients are well combined, pour the mixture back into the saucepan. Cook over moderate heat, stirring constantly and deeply into the sides of the pan with a wooden spoon until the mixture begins to thicken into a light custard that barely coats the spoon. Now lower the heat and continue to cook and stir, raising the pan away from the heat occasionally if it seems to be getting too hot. Under no circumstances allow the custard to boil or it will curdle irretrievably. When the custard is thick enough to cling heavily to the spoon, remove it from the heat and stir in the softened gelatin until it has completely dissolved.

Place the custard in the refrigerator, and stir occasionally to hasten the cooling. If the custard should thicken too much, beat vigorously with a wire whisk. When cool, stir in 2 or 3 tablespoons of Kirsch, according to your taste.

Completing the charlotte. Pour 1½ cups of chilled heavy cream into a large chilled bowl, and beat with a rotary or electric beater until it holds soft peaks.

Pour the cooled custard over the whipped cream, then fold in carefully and thoroughly. Ladle the mixture into the prepared mold with care so as not to disturb the ladyfingers. Smooth the top with a spatula, and cover tightly with plastic wrap. Refrigerate for at least 6 hours, or until firm.

Unmolding and serving the dessert. Place a flat serving platter on top of the charlotte mold. Grasp both platter and mold firmly and invert, then gently lift off the mold.

Although it is not necessary to do so, garnishing the mold makes it particularly attractive. Pour 1 cup of heavy cream into a chilled bowl, and whip it until it is fairly stiff, being careful not to overbeat it. Spoon the whipped cream into a pastry bag fitted with a fluted tube, pipe rosettes all around the edge of the charlotte, then add 1 or 2 candied violets to each rosette.

To serve the charlotte, simply cut into wedges as you would when slicing a cake.

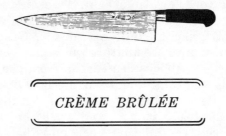

CRÈME BRÛLÉE

Crème brûlée, meaning "burnt cream" but definitely a cold custard, did not, as many people have thought, originate in New Orleans or even France, but, of all places, at Trinity College, Cambridge, England. As a consequence, it is also known as Cambridge cream. Although the English finish crème brûlée with granulated sugar to give it its golden crust, in this country we use light-brown sugar.

SERVES 6

    3 cups light cream
    6 egg yolks
    4 teaspoons granulated sugar
    ⅛ teaspoon salt
    1½ teaspoons vanilla extract
    ¼ cup light-brown sugar, firmly packed

Preheating the oven. Slide an oven shelf into a center slot. Place a roasting pan at least 3 inches deep on the shelf, and add enough hot water from the tap—about 6 to 8 cups—to half-fill the pan. Preheat the oven and the pan of water at 350° F. for at least 15 minutes, or until you are ready to bake the crème.
Making the crème. Pour the light cream into a medium-size heavy

saucepan, and over moderate heat, bring it to the boiling point, or until a film wrinkles over the surface.

Meanwhile, place the egg yolks in a medium-size bowl and beat with a rotary or electric beater until thick, creamy, and pale yellow. Beat in the granulated sugar.

Remove any skin that may have formed on the cream, then, beating constantly with a wire whisk, add the hot cream slowly to the egg yolk mixture. When all the cream has been added, stir in the salt and vanilla. Pour the crème mixture into a 1-quart flame-proof baking dish.

Baking the crème. Place the baking dish in the pan of water in the oven. The hot water should reach to two-thirds the depth of the baking dish; add more hot water if needed. Bake for 20 minutes.

Meanwhile, cut a square of foil large enough to extend be-yond the rim of the baking dish, and cover the crème completely. This forestalls too much browning. Reduce the oven heat to 325° F. and continue baking another 30 to 40 minutes, or until a thin-bladed knife or a skewer inserted 1 inch from the outside edge comes out clean—that is, without any custard clinging to it.

To remove the crème from the oven, pull the oven rack for-ward slowly so as not to splash the hot water on the custard (or yourself). Using potholders, lift the crème from the pan, remove the foil covering, and let the crème cool. Then cover tightly with plastic wrap or fresh foil, and refrigerate until firm. You can, if you like, prepare the recipe to this stage up to 24 hours in advance.

Finishing the crème brûlée. Slide an oven or broiler shelf into a slot 4 to 5 inches from the source of heat, and turn on the broiler at its highest setting to heat for 15 minutes.

Pour ¼ cup of light-brown sugar into a fine sieve and sift it over the surface of the chilled crème as evenly as possible, right to the edges of the bowl.

Place the dish of crème in the center of the shelf in the pre-heated broiler, and broil until the sugar melts and forms a crust. Do not close the oven door, and watch sharply so that the sugar does not burn. You may find it necessary to rotate the dish so that the sugar melts more or less evenly.

Remove the dish from the oven immediately, and refrigerate for about 2 hours. When chilled, the caramelized sugar will be brittle and sound hollow if you tap it with your finger.

Serving the crème brûlée. Be sure each serving contains some of the crunchy caramelized sugar, because it is the major sweetness of this rich dessert.

FILBERT BLANCMANGE WITH FRESH PEACHES

From the French *blanc-manger* (white eating), the cool white dessert cream known as blancmange has been the delight of French gourmets for more than two centuries. Always thickened with gelatin in France, rather than with cornstarch or arrowroot as in America, it is traditionally flavored with almonds. This recipe substitutes filberts for almonds. Blancmange should always be served very cold.

SERVES 6

For Preparing the Mold
1 tablespoon vegetable oil

The Blancmange
2¼ cups cold water
1½ envelopes (1½ tablespoons) unflavored gelatin
1 cup (¼ pound) shelled, blanched filberts
1 to 1¼ cups milk
½ cup sugar
2 to 3 tablespoons light rum

The Peaches
3 ripe peaches or two 10-ounce packages frozen sliced peaches,
    defrosted but not drained
Juice of 1 lemon
2 to 3 tablespoons sugar
1 to 2 tablespoons dark rum

Preparing the mold. Using a pastry brush, lightly coat the inside of a 4- or 5-cup ring mold with the vegetable oil. Turn the mold upside down on paper toweling to allow any excess oil to drain off.
Softening the gelatin. Measure ¼ cup of the cold water into a small cup and sprinkle the unflavored gelatin over the surface to soften. Set aside.
Blanching the filberts. If you are unable to obtain filberts already blanched, blanch them yourself by boiling 10 minutes in enough water to cover. Drain, and while the nuts are still hot, rub briskly in a Turkish towel to remove as much skin as possible.

Making the filbert milk. Place ½ cup of the blanched filberts and 1 cup of the cold water in the container of an electric blender or food processor. Process until the nuts are completely pulverized, in the blender at high speed, and in the food processor using the metal blade and turning on and off rapidly. Place a large sieve over a medium-size bowl and line it with several thicknesses of cheesecloth. Pour the puréed filberts into the sieve.

In the same way, purée the remaining ½ cup of blanched filberts in the remaining 1 cup of water, then add to the sieve. Press the nuts with a rubber spatula or the back of a spoon to speed up the draining. When most of the "filbert milk" has drained through, pick up the cheesecloth and squeeze hard with your hands to extract every last drop of the "milk." Discard the filbert pulp. Measure the "milk." You should have 1¾ to 2 cups. If not, add enough whole milk to make up the difference to 2 cups.

Making the blancmange. In a small heavy saucepan, combine the 2 cups of "filbert milk" with 1 cup of the whole milk, ½ cup sugar, and the softened gelatin. Set over moderate heat and stir constantly just long enough for the sugar and gelatin to dissolve. The mixture must not boil.

Remove from the heat and cool to lukewarm, then stir in 2 to 3 tablespoons of light rum to taste. Keep in mind that when the blancmange is cold, the rum flavor will be considerably less pronounced.

If there is any hint of a film or "skin" on the blancmange mixture, strain it through a very fine sieve directly into the prepared mold. Otherwise, pour into the mold directly. Cover the mold tightly with plastic wrap or foil, and refrigerate for about 4 hours, or until firm and cold.

Preparing the peaches. About ½ hour before serving, peel, pit, and thinly slice the ripe peaches. Place them in a medium-size mixing bowl, add the lemon juice, and toss so that the peach slices are well coated with lemon juice, which will keep them from darkening. Drain off the lemon juice, and add 2 tablespoons of the sugar and 1 tablespoon of the dark rum. Toss to mix, then taste; you may want to add the remaining tablespoon of sugar and/or rum. If using defrosted frozen sliced peaches, simply mix in a little rum to taste; you won't need to add any lemon juice or sugar.

Unmolding and serving the blancmange. Run a small sharp knife around the edge of the mold and around the tube in the center. Then dip the bottom of the mold in a shallow pan of hot water for about a second. Wipe the mold dry, place a chilled serving platter on top of it, and, holding both mold and platter firmly, invert. The blancmange should fall out easily. If not, rap the platter sharply on the table once. If necessary, dip the platter again in hot water.

Fill the center of the blancmange with the sliced peaches and serve.

Culinary Glossary

Here you will find terms and definitions, explanations, discussions of foods and ingredients, and other miscellaneous information pertaining to the recipes in this book.

Baking powder. Baking powder is a chemical leavener, composed of an alkaline substance (baking soda) combined with one or more acid ingredients and a small amount of starch that serves as a stabilizer. When moistened, these ingredients give off carbon dioxide gas that leavens the batters.

Double-acting baking powder is always specified in this book. Single-acting (or tartrate) baking powder begins to release its carbon dioxide gas as soon as it is moistened. On the other hand, double-acting baking powder releases only a fraction of its gas into the batter when moistened, reserving the rest of its leavening power until the batter is exposed to heat.

If you must for any reason use single-acting baking powder, there should not be a moment's delay between the mixing of the batter and baking it if you would have the batter rise to its full height.

Baking soda. Baking soda, also called bicarbonate of soda and sodium bicarbonate, is always used, often together with baking powder, when a batter is made with an acid liquid. When baking soda encounters the acid in buttermilk, sour milk, or sour cream, it reacts in the same way as baking powder does when moistened with an ordinary liquid—it produces carbon dioxide gas that leavens the mixture.

Butter. The U.S. Department of Agriculture grades butter on the basis of such factors as aroma, texture, and flavor. The best butter, made of sweet cream, is scored AA, the next best, A—the packages are so labeled. The butter may be either salted or unsalted. Sweet (unsalted) butter is preferred for all recipes in this book. If you use salted butter, reduce the amount of salt called for by one-half.

Buttermilk. As country folk know it, buttermilk is the liquid that remains after butter has been churned from ripened (soured) cream. Buttermilk that originates in this way is, alas, no longer available in retail markets. What you get when you buy buttermilk today is a cultured product composed of skimmed or partially skimmed milk that has been soured and thickened by a culture of lactic-acid bacteria.

Cultured buttermilk can be purchased everywhere, but individual dairies use different cultures. Not surprisingly, the flavor and the thickness will vary from brand to brand. Often buttermilk will be excessively bland or too thin. For the best results with the recipes in this book, try to find a cultured buttermilk that pours out in a thick, smooth stream and has a definitely acidulated but pleasant flavor.

Cheese. Some cheeses are more suitable for cooking than others. Their usefulness is determined by how easily and smoothly they melt, how much heat they can tolerate, how much flavor and character they retain, and how well they combine with other foods. Parmesan and Gruyère are unquestionably the greatest cooking cheeses in the world.

Parmesan behaves most predictably. No matter to what degree of heat it is subjected, Parmesan seldom turns stringy, and its flavor remains constant and incomparable. Since the name "Parmesan" is not protected by law in the United States, you must learn to recognize the characteristic smoky black rind, the pale golden yellow color, the closely grained texture, and the sweet piquant taste of authentic Parmesan. The older the cheese, the better its flavor. Moreover, it makes lighter-than-air cheese soufflés even lighter, and gives gratinéed dishes a finer crust and better flavor than buttered bread crumbs or grated Gruyère alone ever did.

Switzerland cheese—the authentic cheese is always called Switzerland cheese and not Swiss cheese—has many varieties and many imitators. True Switzerland cheese is identified by its name stenciled all over its rind. The three varieties imported in significant quantities are Emmenthal, the most popular, which has the largest eyes and a nutty, distinctly sweet flavor; Gruyère, with holes the size of peas, and more tartness and bite; and Appenzell, with almost imperceptible holes and the most intense flavor of the three. For the recipes in this book, Gruyère is preferred. Young Switzerland cheeses are blander than aged cheeses, and they don't melt as well as older ones.

Corn meal. See Flour.

Corn syrup. See Sugars and sweeteners.

Cream. When a recipe specifies heavy cream (sweet cream), called whipping cream in some parts of the country, it means cream with a butterfat content of at least 30 percent.

MAKING WHIPPED CREAM. Chill the cream, the bowl, and the beaters before whipping, then follow the instructions in individual recipes as to whether the cream is to be whipped until stiff, or just until it holds its shape in soft peaks.

To pipe whipped cream rosettes, whip the cream until stiff, and use a canvas pastry bag, which will grip the cream better than will a nylon pastry bag. To fill the bag, turn the top back as you would a cuff, drop the metal tip in place, and spoon in the whipped cream to half-fill the bag. Gather the top of the bag with one hand, then squeeze the bag with the other hand, forcing the cream out.

Eggs. When recipes in this book call for eggs, "large" eggs, which weigh 24 ounces to the dozen, are specified. Substitutions of small (18 ounces per dozen), medium (21 ounces), extra large (27 ounces), or jumbo (30 ounces) eggs may upset the balance created to ensure the success of the recipes.

In most recipes the freshness of the eggs is of less importance than their size, but when freshness is of critical importance, or, conversely, when eggs a few days old are desirable, it is indicated in the recipe.

As for color, it matters not at all if the eggs are brown or white; there is absolutely no difference in quality or flavor between them.

SEPARATING EGGS. Use three bowls—one for the yolks, one for the whites, and a small bowl over which you separate each egg, thus eliminating the possibility of breaking a yolk into the bowl of whites. Whites will not beat up properly if they contain even so much as a drop of yolks or, for that matter, any fat.

To separate an egg, crack the shell at its midcenter sharply on the edge of the small bowl. Pull the two halves apart, holding them upright, over the bowl. The yolk, because it is heavier, will automatically remain in one half, while the white will run out. Switch the yolk back and forth between the shells until all the white has disengaged itself and dropped into the small bowl. Then pour the white into the bowl in which you intend to beat the whites. Drop the yolk into its proper bowl.

If you should break a yolk and even a small amount of it falls into the white, lift it out with a piece of shell or paper toweling. If you are unable to retrieve all of the yolk, discard the egg (or use it for another purpose).

BEATING EGG WHITES. When properly beaten, egg whites mount to seven or eight times their original volume. They are smooth and glistening, sometimes called "wet," free from granules, and will hold firm, glossy peaks when the beater is lifted straight up. If they are granular or dry, they have been overbeaten, much of the air will have been lost, and soufflés particularly will not rise properly. It is the air beaten into egg whites that expands as a soufflé bakes, giving it its impressive height.

You might note that whatever else you may have heard, there is little difference in volume and stiffness between egg whites at room temperature and those that are cold when you beat them.

For whipping egg whites, traditionalists recommend the big balloon whip (*fouet*, in French) and an unlined copper bowl, with which egg whites mount faster and with greater volume. The chemical reaction that takes place because of the copper affects the whites in some mysterious manner so that soufflés rise higher than you ever dreamed possible. If you don't have a copper bowl (and it's worth the investment if you are a serious cook), use a glass or stainless-steel bowl; do not use aluminum, which will turn the whites gray, or plastic, which is likely to decrease their volume. If you prefer not to beat by hand, modern beaters —the rotary, the portable electric, and the big electric mixer—are marvelously effective pieces of equipment.

FOLDING EGG WHITES INTO A HEAVIER MIXTURE. Folding means to

combine a fragile mixture such as beaten egg whites with a heavier mixture, such as a soufflé base or batter. To do this, add about a cup of the beaten whites to the heavier mixture and whip them in vigorously with a wire whip or whisk. This lightens the mixture and makes folding easier. Then, using a rubber spatula, scoop the mixture on top of the remaining egg whites. Still using a rubber spatula, cut down from the top center of the mixture to the very bottom of the bowl, then draw the spatula toward you against the edge of the bowl, rotating the bowl as you work. Working quickly, repeat this cutting and folding until the whites have been folded in, but do not try to be too thorough, especially in making a soufflé; better to have a few unblended patches of egg white than a soufflé that won't rise.

Flour. Simply stated, flour is fine, often powdery meal obtained by grinding an edible grain. Although flour can be made of any grain in addition to wheat—rye, rice, or corn, for example, or even from legumes or roots—the flour most commonly used is made from wheat.

Wheat flour is available in many varieties—bread flour, bleached or unbleached all-purpose flour, cake flour, whole-wheat flour, instant or granulated flour, self-rising flour (actually a mix), and others—each one composed of hard winter wheat or soft spring wheat, or a combination of the two in various proportions.

All wheat flours have at least one element in common: gluten. When flour is moistened and mixed, gluten is developed in the dough from two protein substances in the flour—gliadin and glutenin. Since hard wheat has a much higher gluten content than soft wheat, the type of flour you use and to what point you allow its gluten to develop will affect to a significant degree the quality and texture of your crêpes, pancakes, and waffles. If you overmix the batter, you will develop too much gluten, which will make the batter too elastic and the finished product tough.

ALL-PURPOSE FLOUR. Milled from a mixture of hard and soft wheats, all-purpose flour has a moderate gluten content. It is available throughout the United States and sold under many brand names. They all look alike (except for a difference in the degree of whiteness between bleached and unbleached all-purpose flours), but they have subtly different characteristics that are often neither described on their labels nor apparent to the eye: varying proportions of hard and soft wheat, the presence or absence of enrichment, the various processes by which each brand is milled.

To assure you of as much predictability as possible, the recipes that call for all-purpose flour are based on the same brand (Gold Medal) consistently, not because of any intrinsic superiority of that flour to other all-purpose flours, but simply because it is readily available throughout the country.

CAKE FLOUR. This is finely milled white flour made from soft wheat. Cake flour has a low gluten content, so the danger of toughness from overmixing is minimal. No matter what instructions may appear on box labels, it should not be used when all-purpose flour is called for—at least not in these recipes. Make sure that you don't mistakenly buy cake flour labeled "self-rising"; this, like self-rising all-purpose flour, contains baking powder and salt and should under no circumstances be substituted in these recipes.

WHOLE-WHEAT FLOUR (GRAHAM FLOUR). Whole-wheat flour, as is obvious from its name, is milled from whole grain. It is often called graham flour because its use was widely promoted by the vegetarian Sylvester Graham in the early nineteenth century.

Whole-wheat flour is a powerhouse of vitamins, minerals, and other nutrients, and it has a high gluten content. It has a distinctive nutlike flavor because the germ and the bran of the wheat kernel are not removed as they are in the milling of white flour. Stone-ground whole-wheat flour, which is ground between millstones, has far more flavor than flour that is milled by machine.

You might note that whole-wheat flour is quite perishable because of its fat content and should not be purchased if you have reason to believe that it has been in stock longer than a month or so. And you should use it fairly promptly; it has a shelf life of only about 4 months.

Gelatin. Commercial gelatin in powdered form is sold in the United States in envelopes. Each envelope equals ¼ ounce (1 tablespoon). The gelatin may be softened in a small amount of liquid before being added to other ingredients, or it may be combined with other dry ingredients first. The proportion of gelatin to liquid varies in each recipe, depending on the dish.

Margarine. Margarine is made by emulsifying oil—usually vegetable oil, although some margarines contain animal fats—with cultured milk, then kneading the resulting fat to a consistency similar to that of butter. Margarine has no flavor except what it gains from being churned with the milk, plus artificial flavorings. Because of this, the recipes in this book do not call for margarine. If, however, butter is dietetically prohibited, margarine may be substituted in all these recipes.

Potatoes. The amount of starch a potato contains is the crucial factor. A potato with a low starch content—loosely categorized as a boiling potato—is most likely to remain firm after cooking. A potato with a high starch content—loosely categorized as a baking potato—will be mealier and fluffier than the boiling type, and it is more likely to fall apart when boiled. It is difficult to identify boiling and baking potatoes by sight, but it is helpful to remember that mature, or old, potatoes, whatever their type, contain more starch than young, new potatoes.

Ribbons. When egg yolks and sugar are beaten together to perfect consistency, the mixture becomes pale yellow and thick enough, when dropped from a raised beater, to fall back on itself, making "ribbons" that disappear slowly into the mixture.

Sour cream. Sour cream, like buttermilk, is a commercially cultured product. Light cream (cream containing from 18 to 20 percent butterfat) is homogenized and pasteurized, then mixed with a lactic-acid bacteria culture and allowed to ripen until it reaches the desired thickness and degree of acidulation.

Cultured sour cream, like cultured buttermilk, varies in flavor from one dairy to another. Some brands have more body than others when newly made. Sour cream stored in the refrigerator never thins out, but continues to thicken as it stands. Its staying power when properly refrigerated is quite remarkable—it will keep for at least a week. Should you notice an accumulation of watery fluid in the container, simply pour it off before measuring the sour cream.

Spinach. A quick and easy way to stem spinach is to lay a few spinach leaves in one hand with the undersides up, then fold the leaves over. Holding the folded spinach leaves firmly, grasp the stems with the other hand and with a short, quick jerk, pull the stems out.

Stocks and broths. If you lack freshly made chicken or beef stock, a good canned brand—always called broth, incidentally, on the can—will serve almost as well. If the canned broth is a condensed type, follow the directions on the can for diluting with water. There are, however, brands of chicken and beef broth that do not call for any dilution. These, for the most part, are superior to the condensed broths.

Don't use canned consommé, either chicken or beef, as a substitute for broth. Canned consommés are generally too sweet in flavor and may contain added gelatin.

Sugars and sweeteners. When sugar is listed in this book without further description, ordinary granulated white sugar, made from sugar beet or cane, is meant; other sweeteners are indicated by name.

BROWN SUGAR. Brown sugar, both light and dark, has molasses added in varying amounts. When a recipe calls for brown sugar, do not use granulated brown (or Brownulated) sugar, which pours easily but behaves rather unpredictably in cooking.

SUPERFINE SUGAR. Finely granulated white sugar, sometimes called instant sugar, this is used mainly in desserts and drinks.

CONFECTIONERS' SUGAR. This fine-textured sugar, which contains about 3 percent cornstarch to prevent caking, is used mainly in frostings or for dusting the tops of soufflés and cakes. It is frequently called "powdered sugar," but the label on the box may read 10X Confectioners' Sugar or XXXX.

Wines and spirits. When wine is included among the ingredients in a recipe, under no circumstances use so-called cooking wine or a wine that you wouldn't drink. It will taste just as bad in the dish as it would in a glass. Any good domestic wine will do, and only if you feel extravagant need you use an imported wine.

Less familiar forms of wine cookery employ the aristocratic fortified wines; that is, wines fortified after fermentation with added alcohol or brandy. Of them all, port, Madeira, and Marsala are the finest for cooking. Unlike table wines, most fortified wines should never be cooked for any length of time because intense heat destroys their penetrating and distinctive bouquet. If they are heated to just below the boiling point, all taste of alcohol will be gone and the wines will bloom at their peak of flavor.

Heavily sweetened liqueurs are generally effective in desserts such as soufflés. These may be flavored with almost any sweet liqueur, and the most popular is surely Grand Marnier, but don't overlook more unusual liqueur flavors like crème de cacao. Their flavors are so concentrated that only a small amount of a liqueur, whatever its flavor, is needed to achieve the desired effect.

FLAMING FOODS. High alcohol content is necessary for effective flaming. A spirit—whether it is Cognac distilled from wine, Calvados from apples, gin from grain, rum from sugar cane, or aquavit from potatoes—more than meets this requirement; it contains at least 40 percent alcohol by volume, or 80 proof as we describe it in the United States.

Although it is not necessary or even desirable that the spirit be fully cooked, it is imperative that the alcohol be allowed to burn itself out completely because any alcohol remaining will insidiously penetrate the food and give it an almost medicinal aftertaste. Thorough flaming is best accomplished by heating the spirit to lukewarm in a small pan before lighting it, and whenever appropriate to the dish—flambéed crêpes, for example—first sprinkling the food with a little sugar to add extra fuel to the flame.

Metric Equivalents
of Weights and Measures

As you convert to the metric system, you will find that in cooking, three kinds of measurements are affected by the change: weight, in which the basic measure will be the gram (g.); temperature, which will be expressed in degrees Celsius (° C.), also called Centigrade; and volume, in which the basic metric unit is the liter (l.). Until you actually start thinking in metric units, the following conversion tables of approximate equivalents will help you find your way between the two systems.

Weight

To convert ounces to grams, multiply by 28.35.
To convert grams to ounces, multiply by 0.035.
To convert pounds to kilograms, multiply by 0.45.
To convert kilograms to pounds, multiply by 2.2.

OUNCES/POUNDS	GRAMS/KILOGRAMS
¼ oz.	7.1 g.
½ oz.	14.17 g.
¾ oz.	21.27 g.
1 oz.	28.35 g.
¼ lb. (4 oz.)	.113 kg. (113 g.)
½ lb.	.227 kg.
¾ lb.	.340 kg.
1 lb.	.454 kg.
2.2 lb.	1 kg.

Temperature

To convert degrees Fahrenheit to degrees Celsius, subtract 32, multiply by 5, and divide by 9.

To convert degrees Celsius to degrees Fahrenheit, multiply by 9, divide by 5, and add 32.

OVEN TEMPERATURES

° F.	° C.	Description
160	71	Warm
170	77	
200	93	
205	96	Simmer
212	100	Boil
225	107	Very slow
250	121	
275	135	
300	149	Slow
325	163	
350	177	Moderate
375	190	
400	204	Hot
425	218	
450	232	
475	246	Very hot
500	260	
525	274	
550	288	

Volume

To convert U.S. quarts to liters, multiply by 0.95.
To convert liters to U.S. quarts, multiply by 1.057.
To convert gallons to liters, multiply by 3.8.
To convert liters to gallons, multiply by 0.26.
To convert pints to liters, multiply by 0.47.
To convert liters to pints, multiply by 2.13.
To convert cups to liters, multiply by 0.24.
To convert liters to cups, multiply by 4.17.
To convert teaspoons to milliliters, multiply by 5.
To convert milliliters to teaspoons, multiply by 0.20.
To convert tablespoons to milliliters, multiply by 15.
To convert milliliters to tablespoons, multiply by 0.07.
To convert fluid ounces to milliliters, multiply by 30.
To convert milliliters to fluid ounces, multiply by 0.03.

LIQUID MEASURE	MILLILITERS
¼ teaspoon	1.25 ml.
½ teaspoon	2.5 ml.
¾ teaspoon	3.75 ml.
1 teaspoon	5 ml.
1 tablespoon	15 ml.
¼ fluid ounce	7.5 ml.
½ fluid ounce	15 ml.
1 fluid ounce	30 ml.
¼ cup	59 ml.
⅓ cup	78 ml.
½ cup	118 ml.
⅔ cup	157 ml.
¾ cup	177 ml.
1 cup	236 ml. or .24 liter
½ pint	236 ml. or .24 liter
1 pint	473 ml. or .47 liter
1 quart	946 ml. or .95 liter
1 gallon	3785 ml. or 3.8 liters

Index

Oil(s)
  olive, in Italian omelets, 10
  vegetable, as ingredient in bat-
    ters, 35
Omelet(s)
  bacon, 13
  cheese, 13
    puffed, 18–20
  chicken liver, 13
  crabmeat, 13
  crouton, 13
  French
    filled, 13–14
    scrambled, 12–13
    scrambled with red caviar and
      sour cream, 14
  herbed, 13
  ingredients for, 10–11
  Italian
    with artichoke hearts and
      Parmesan cheese, 16
    with croutons and mozzarella
      cheese, 17–18
    with zucchini and Parmesan
      cheese, 15–16
  lobster, 13
  mushroom, 13
  pans
    to butter, 11
    to heat, 11
  puffed
    cheese, 18–20
    pineapple-filled, 21–22
    sweet, 20
    techniques for making, 10, 11
  to serve, 11
  shrimp, 14
  size of, 11
  soufflé, 132–33
  techniques for making, 9–10, 11
Onion soufflé with Swedish meat-
    balls and cream sauce, 116–
    20
Orange(s)
  butter sauce, flambéed crêpes
    with, 66–67

chocolate-, mousse, 165–67
pudding soufflé with orange
    sauce, 141–44
-pumpkin mousse, 167–69
rind, candied, to make, 169
sauce, orange pudding soufflé
    with, 141–44
Oven thermometers, 6
Oyster soufflé, 108–10

Palacsintak Barackizzel, 90–92
Palatschinka, 90–92
Pan(s)
  for bain–marie, 3
  crêpe, 3
    to heat, 37
  frying, 3
    electric, 2
    to heat, for pancakes, 71
  jelly-roll, 3
  omelet
    to butter, 11
    to heat, 11
  roasting, 3
  saucepans, 3
  sauté, 3
Pancake(s)
  American, 72–75
    accompaniments for, 72–73
  apple, 87–89
  apricot, Hungarian, 90–92
  batter
    to keep, 71
    to measure, 71
    to mix, 70–71
  blueberry, 77–79
  buttermilk, 75–76
  cherry, 89
  to cook, 71–72
  cottage-cheese, 79–80
  to heat pan or griddle for, 71
  potato
    crispy, 84–87
    German, 82–84
  to serve, 72
  spinach, 80–82